Too Cute Crochet
for Babies & Toddlers

A Whimsical Collection of Hats, Scarves,
Mittens & Booties

Too Cute Crochet for Babies & Toddlers

A Whimsical Collection of Hats, Scarves, Mittens & Booties

Cynthia Preston

A Division of Sterling Publishing Co., Inc.
New York

EDITOR
Joanne O'Sullivan

ART DIRECTOR
Stacey Budge

PHOTOGRAPHY
Sandra Stambaugh

ILLUSTRATOR
August Hoerr

COVER DESIGNER
Barbara Zaretsky

CROCHET CONSULTANT
Marilyn Hastings

ASSOCIATE ART DIRECTOR
Shannon Yokeley

EDITORIAL ASSISTANCE
Delores Gosnell

DEDICATION

To all needle workers. In this high-tech age, needlework done by hand is a balm and blessing. No machine can match the wonderful feeling of something made by hand. Let's preserve the "gentle arts" for generations to come.

Library of Congress Cataloging-in-Publication Data

Preston, Cynthia, 1951-
Too cute crochet for babies and toddlers : a whimsical collection of hats, scarves, mittens & booties / by Cynthia Preston.
p. cm.
Includes index.
ISBN 1-57990-581-1 (pbk.)
1. Crocheting--Patterns. 2. Infant's clothing. I. Title.
TT825.P74 2005
746.43'40432--dc22
2004017913

10 9 8 7 6 5 4 3 2

Published by Lark Books, A Division of
Sterling Publishing Co., Inc.
387 Park Avenue South, New York, N.Y. 10016

Distributed in Canada by Sterling Publishing,
c/o Canadian Manda Group, 165 Dufferin Street
Toronto, Ontario, Canada M6K 3H6

Distributed in the U.K. by Guild of Master Craftsman Publications Ltd., Castle Place,
166 High Street, Lewes, East Sussex, England BN7 1XU
Tel: (+ 44) 1273 477374, Fax: (+ 44) 1273 478606,
e-mail: pubs@thegmcgroup.com, Web: www.gmcpublications.com

Distributed in Australia by Capricorn Link (Australia) Pty Ltd.,
P.O. Box 704, Windsor, NSW 2756 Australia

If you have questions or comments about this book, please contact:
Lark Books
67 Broadway
Asheville, NC 28801
(828) 253-0467

Manufactured in China

ISBN 1-57990-581-1

For information about custom editions, special sales, premium and corporate purchases, please contact Sterling Special Sales Department at 800-805-5489 or specialsales@sterlingpub.com.

CONTENTS

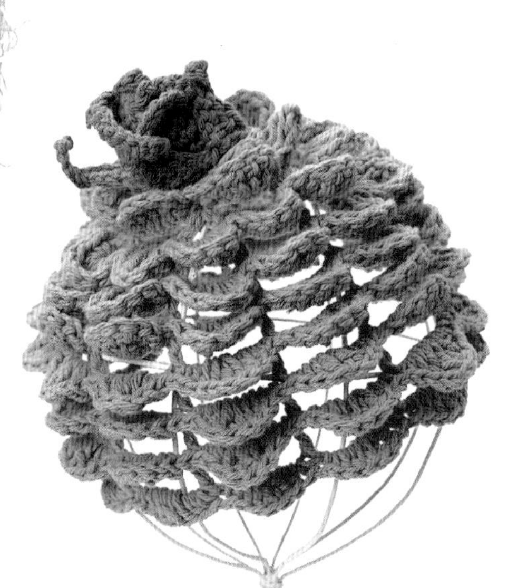

Introduction

A baby always draws warm smiles and coos from admirers, but a baby in a pointy elf hat? He draws a crowd! There's something irresistible about little ones transformed by hats, mitts, and booties into cuddly animals, delicate flowers, or even fruits or vegetables. They're adorable and silly in the sweetest possible way. For a crocheter, making handmade baby items can be among the most rewarding projects. I hope the patterns in this book will prove that they can also be among the most fun to make.

I learned crochet from my Sicilian Nana when I was about eight years old. After trying sewing and knitting in grade school, I went back to crocheting, first learning granny squares, then moving on to three-dimensional objects. When I started making baby hats, the response was overwhelming. People, especially moms, love the hats, and that makes creating them even more enjoyable. After I made the first designs, I started getting suggestions for new ones—"How about a daisy? A calf? An eggplant?" Something about them inspires imagination and creativity!

You'll also find that each hat has its own unique energy and personality, just like the child who wears it—your niece may definitely be a strawberry, while your neighbor's son is unquestionably a cowboy. There are plenty of designs to choose from—charming, costume-like creations from the Whimsical Characters section, flowers from the Garden Delights section, baby animals from the Lovable Zoo section, fruits and veggies from the Fresh Picks section, and delicious confections from the Sweet Treats section. You're bound to find just the right look for the unique baby or toddler in your life. Plus, there's a range of projects for a range of crochet skills, from beginner to advanced.

When making the patterns, don't be afraid to experiment with your own ideas—try different yarns or colors, or add your own special details. And try not to take your work too seriously—celebrate the playful spirit of these crowd-pleasing hats!

I hope that you'll enjoy making these projects as much as I did. There's nothing like the first time a child wears her crocheted hat and mitts, and everyone in the room reacts with "oohs" and "aahs," then reaches for a camera. I really wish Nana could see what I've done—I'm sure she would be pleased.

Getting Started

In designing the projects for this book, I tried to come up with something for everyone. There are easy projects made with basic stitches for beginners and plenty of patterns that combine unusual stitches for those with more skills. Even the most advanced crocheter can find designs that offer new challenges. Most of the hats and accessories can be made in just a few hours.

The following section is a reference guide to turn to as you work and encounter new stitches or unfamiliar terms, or just need a reminder for stitches you haven't tried in a while.

BASIC STITCHES

If you've crocheted before, you're familiar with these basic stitches, but less experienced crocheters may want to use the following section as a refresher course.

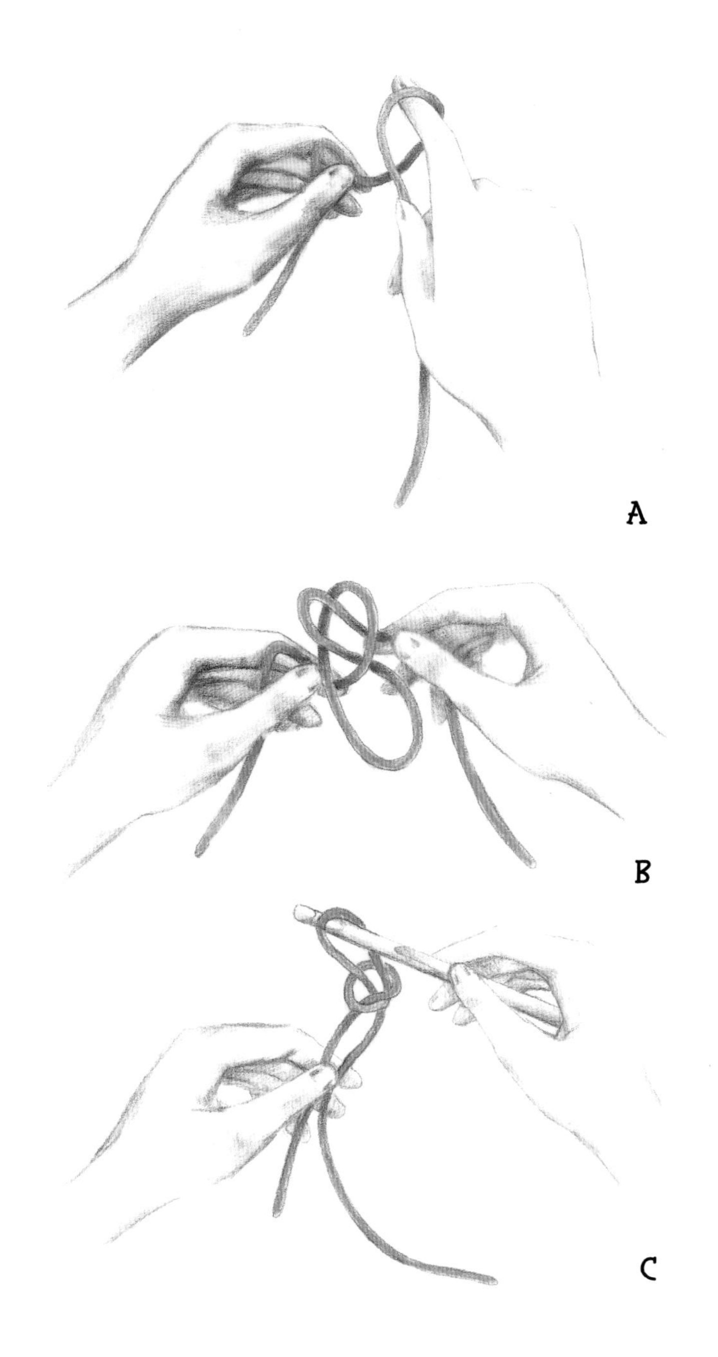

Making a Slip Knot

Almost every crochet project is begun by making a slip knot and then a chain. This is the "foundation" chain that you will make your first row of crochet stitches into. To make a slip knot, you hold the tail of the yarn in your left hand and wrap the yarn around your right pointer finger as shown (A). Push a second loop up through the bottom of the first loop (B). Put your hook through the new loop. Hold onto both ends of yarn and pull the knot snugly up to the hook, but not too tight! You will want to be able to slide it off the hook later (C).

Crochet Hook Sizes

Crochet hooks sizes may vary slightly from company to company, so test your gauge to make sure that the hook you're using produces the gauge specified for the project.

U.S.	MM	U.K.
D/3	3.25	10
E/4	3.5	9
F/5	3.75	8
G/6	4	7
H/8	5	6
I /9	5.5	5

Abbreviations

beg............. begin, beginning
ch.............. chain
ch sp........... chain space
dc.............. double crochet
dec............. decrease
ea.............. each
hdc............. half-double crochet
hk.............. hook
inc............. increase
loop st......... loop stitch
overlay st...... overlay stitch
rc.............. reverse single crochet
sc.............. single crochet
sl st........... slip stitch
sk.............. skip
sp.............. space
st.............. stitch
st marker....... stitch marker
tog............. together
tr.............. triple crochet
yo.............. yarn over

Note on Instructions

Asterisks

In the instructions for many projects, you'll find asterisks surrounding part of the text. Asterisks are a common convention in crochet instructions; they mean repeat the instructions between asterisks.

Place Marker

The instruction place marker indicates where to slip an open-ended marker into the completed stitch, marking the beginning or the end of the round. Move up as each round is completed.

Making a Chain (ch)

To make a chain, first make a slip knot (see page 11). With the hk through the slip knot, wrap the yarn around the hk (yo), and pull it through the slip knot (loop). Repeat this step to make the number of chain stitches indicated in the instructions.

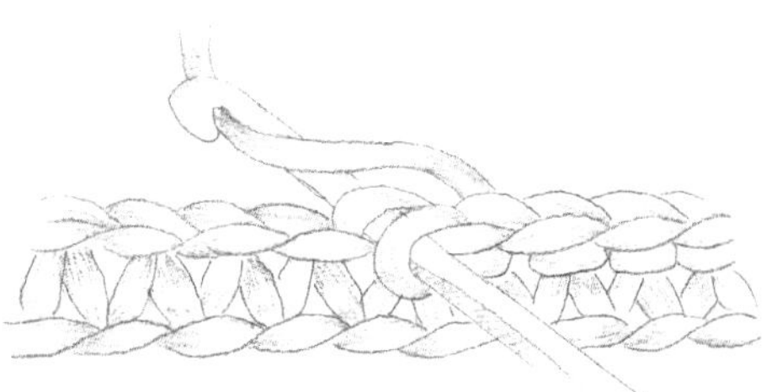

Slip Stitch (sl st)

Push the hk through the second ch from the hk (1 ch and 1 loop on hk). Wrap the yarn around the hk (yo), and pull through both loops on the hk (1 loop remains on hk). Repeat.

Single Crochet (sc)

Push the hk through the second ch from the hk (1 chain and 1 loop on hook). *Yo and pull through the ch (2 loops on hk). Yo again, and pull through both loops on the hk (1 loop remains on hk)*.

Double Crochet (dc)

Yo, insert the hk through the fourth ch from the hk (1 ch and 2 loops on hk). Yo and pull through the ch (3 loops on hk). Yo and pull through 2 loops on the hk (2 loops on hk). Yo and pull through the last 2 loops on the hk (1 loop remains on hk).

Crochet Stitch Names

Crochet stitches have different names on each side of "the big pond." Here's a translation guide.

North American Terms	European Equivalents
slip stitch (sl st)	single crochet
single crochet (sc)	double crochet
half-double crochet (hdc)	half-treble crochet
double crochet (dc)	treble crochet
triple crochet (tr)	double treble

Half-Double Crochet

Yo, insert hk into the fourth ch from the hk. Yo and pull through ch (3 loops remain on the hk). Yo and pull through all three loops at once.

SPECIALTY STITCHES AND TECHNIQUES

Beyond the basic stitches, there are lots of great specialty stitches you can use to create interesting effects in your work.

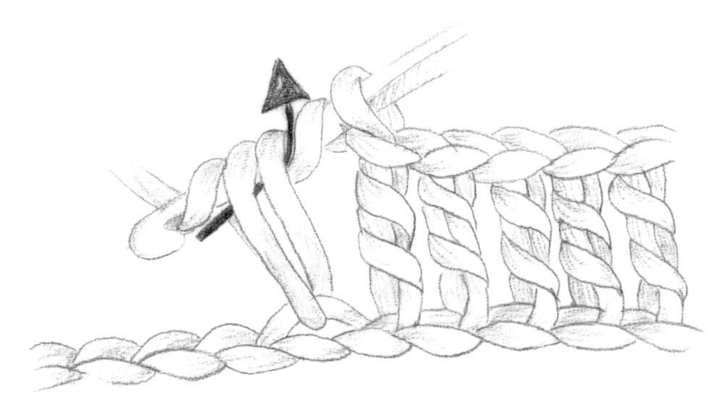

Triple Crochet (tr)

(Used for: Squirrel's Best Friend Hat, Rose Fairy Hat, Fresh-Picked Strawberry Hat, Tiny Eggplant Hat)

Yo hk 2 times, insert hk into fifth ch from hk, yo, draw through ch, (4 loops should be on hk), yo and draw through next 2 loops, yo and draw loop through 2 loops, and yo and draw through 2 loops.

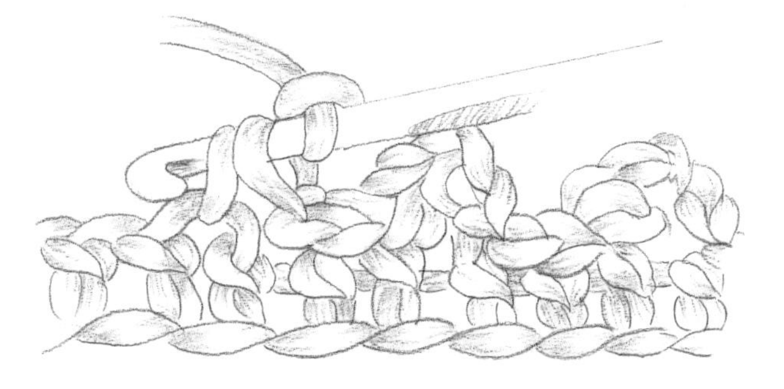

Picot Stitch

(Used for: Petite Prince or Princess, Rose Fairy Hat, Sweet Violet Hat, Darling Daisy Hat and Purse, Squirrel's Best Friend Hat, Tiny Eggplant Hat Mitts, Frisky Whiskers Cat Hat, Friendly Lion Hat)

Ch 3, *go back into base of first ch (or top of slst), sl st. Sc in next st*. This stitch can be formed with 2, 3, 4, or 5 chains.

Pineapple Stitch

(Used for: Squirrel's Best Friend Hat)

On the first row, sk 2 ch, yo, insert the hk into the third ch from the hk, *yo and draw loop up on hk 4 times, yo, draw through 8 loops, yo, draw through 2 loops*, ch 1, sk ch. Repeat. Ch 3 at end of row. On the following rows, make the group in the ch sp between the groups of the previous row.

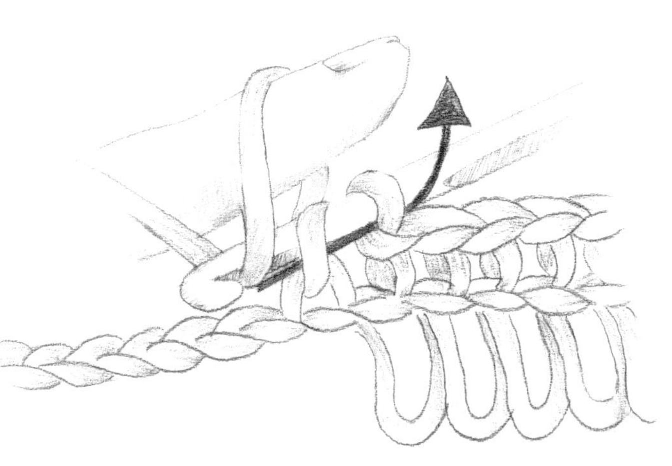

Loop Stitch

ROW OR ROUND 1: Sc in the second ch from hk. Sc in ea ch to end of row. Ch 1, turn.

ROW OR ROUND 2: Sk first st. *Insert hk in next st. Place yarn around middle finger of left hand. Draw yarn through st. Yo and pull through 2 loops. Slip long loop off finger. Continue, keeping loops the same size*. Ch 1, turn.

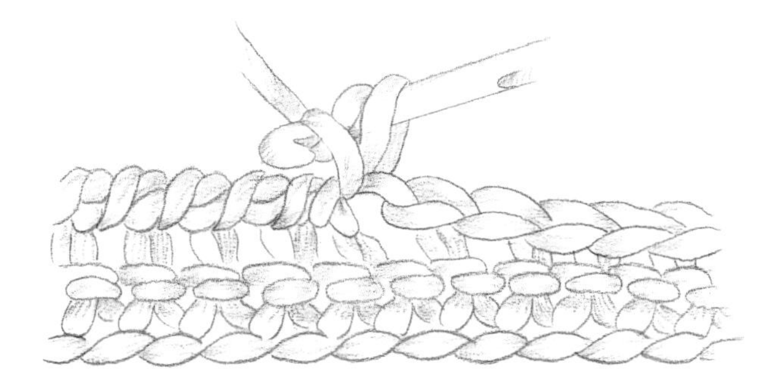

Reverse Single Crochet (rc)

(Used for: Petite Prince or Princess Hat, Tiny Eggplant Hat and Mitts, Fresh-Picked Strawberry Hat, Fifi the Poodle Hat and Mitts, Swiss Miss Hat, Pear-fectly Lovely Hat, Single Scoop Hat)

Work 1 row of sc, then, working form left to right instead right to left, work in sc, insert the hk under both horizontal threads.

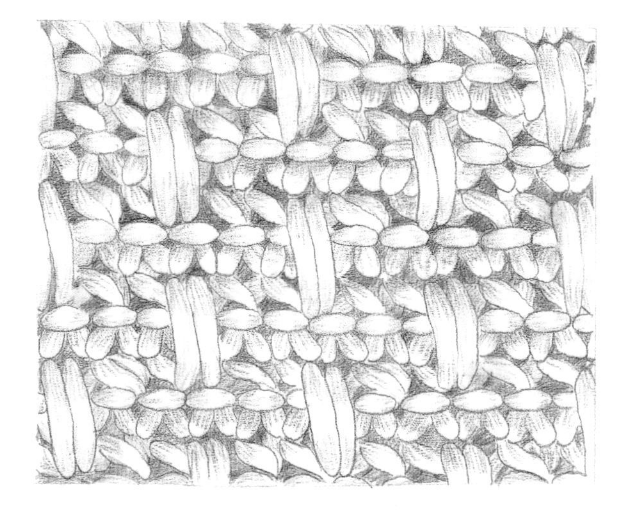

Overlay Stitch

Overlay stitches are graduated loops of sc over crocheted sections. To make them, take a long sc in the indicated sc into the row below it.

Make the long sc as long as the rows below it that you are going over. Yo and pull through as much yarn as needed. Finish the st as if it were sc.

Increases

To increase, insert hk twice in the same st to make two sts.

Decreases

Yo and pick up st, then yo and pick up second st, yo again and pull through 3 loops, instead of 1. Two sts now become one.

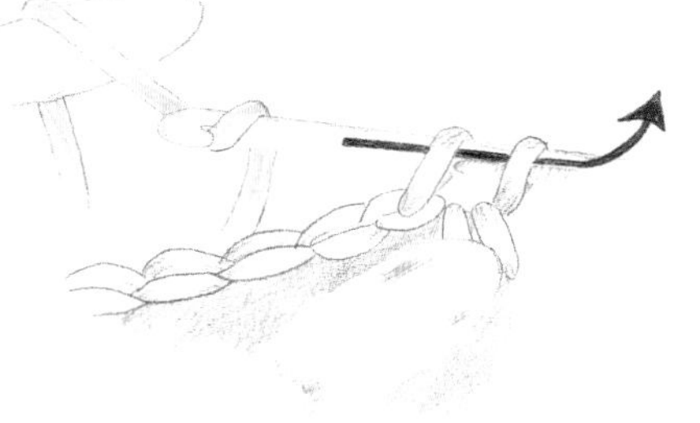

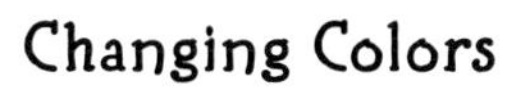

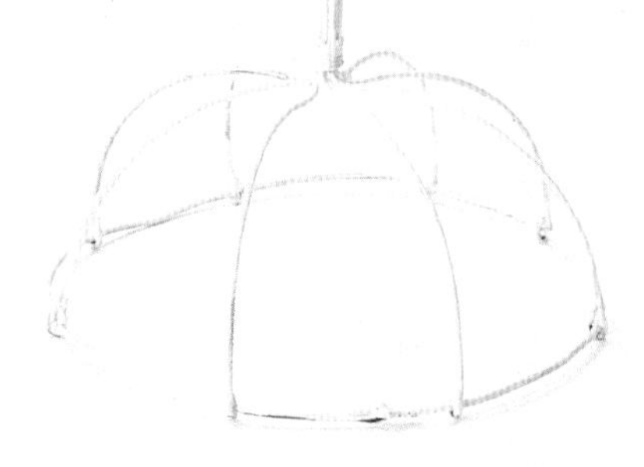

Changing Colors

To change colors on the same row, start your new color at the last step of the last st (2 loops on the hk), pick up the second color and pull it through the loop on the hk, completing the st. Carry the first color along loosely in the back of the work or sc around and on top of it if you're going to use it again in the same row. Complete the last st of the second color with the first color when changing back.

Joining Yarn

When joining yarn, try to avoid knotting it. Crochet your last st in the first yarn up to the last step: in other words, don't fully complete the st with the first yarn, then pull the new yarn through to complete the st. Leave about 4 inches (10 cm) of each yarn on the wrong side to be woven in later.

Shells

Shells are groups of stitches that are made all in one space. They can be made in any stitch, such as double or triple crochet, and there can be any number of stitches in a shell.

Spiral Down

When working in the round, instead of joining the end of round to beg with a sl st, then a ch to go up to next row, you can spiral. Simply mark the first st of the row with a st marker, a piece of contrasting yarn, or hairpin, then crochet the next st. Continue working in rounds and moving first st marker up to each new round's first st. This will prevent a change in pattern of the sts, will be seamless, and will make your work go faster.

Loose Ends

When you fasten off at the end of a color or project (or at the beginning of a project) be sure to leave a tail of yarn long enough to hide well. I usually leave a tail of about 3 to 4 inches (8 to 10 cm) and weave in the ends really well with a hk or tapestry needle. Not doing so cost me a blue ribbon for a crocheted purse I entered in the Jefferson County Fair!

Baby Sizing Table

It's hard to approximate sizes for babies—just like grown ups, they vary greatly. If you are in doubt about the size to make a hat, mitts, or booties, make them larger than you think they should be. The baby will eventually get bigger!

The following chart give size approximates, just to give you an idea of where to start.

	Head circumference	Hands	Feet
Newborn	14 in. (35.6 cm)	2 1/2 in. (6.4 cm)	3 in. (7.6 cm)
1 to 3 Months	16 in. (40.6 cm)	2 1/2 in. (6.4 cm)	3 in. (7.6 cm)
3 to 6 Months	17 in. (43.2 cm)	3 in. (7.6 cm)	3 1/2 in. (8.9 cm)
6 to 9 Months	18 in. (45.7 cm)	3 1/2 in. (8.9 cm)	4 in. (10.2 cm)
9 to 12 Months	19 in. (48.3 cm)	4 1/2 in. (11.4 cm)	5 in. (12.7 cm)
12 to 36 Months	20 to 23 in. (50.8 to 58.4 cm)	5 to 7 in. (12.7 to 18 cm)	5 1/2 to 8 in. (14 to 20.3 cm)

EMBROIDERY AND SEWING STITCHES

Simple embroidery over your crocheted item can personalize it and give it even more depth. When you assemble items with multiple pieces of crochet work, you'll also need to know a few sewing stitches to fasten the pieces together. Both the embroidery and sewing stitches are made using a tapestry needle.

Running Stitch

This is the simplest stitch, used for creating straight lines of any length. Simply bring the tapestry needle through the wrong to the right side of your work and stitch, making a stitch to the desired length, then bring the needle back through.

Daisy Stitch

Bring the needle to the right side of the material. Hold down the thread with your thumb so that a loop will form. Insert the needle at the spot where the thread emerged. Bring it up a short distance from this point. When the thread is drawn through, reinsert the needle, making a small stitch over the end of the loop to hold the loop stitch in place.

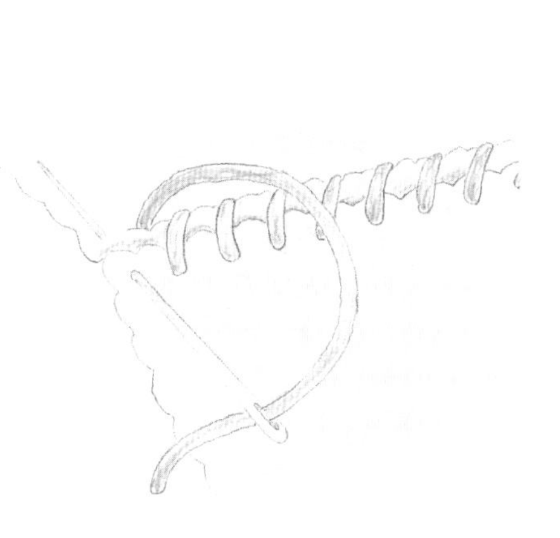

Whipstitch

Insert the needle into the crochet work, over the top of the edge, and back around, repeating as many times as necessary. This stitch is good for sewing two crocheted pieces together.

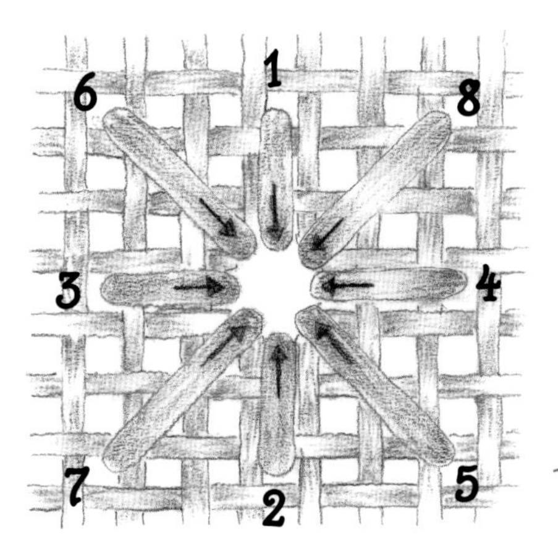

Algerian Eyelet Stitch

Follow the numbers and arrows on the diagram to create a star shape, which can be used to represent flowers, or a number of other motifs.

Back Stitch

This stitch is good for reinforcing the seam between two pieces of crochet work, as well as for embroidering. Insert the needle, bring it out a stitch behind, then insert it a stitch ahead.

EMBELLISHMENTS

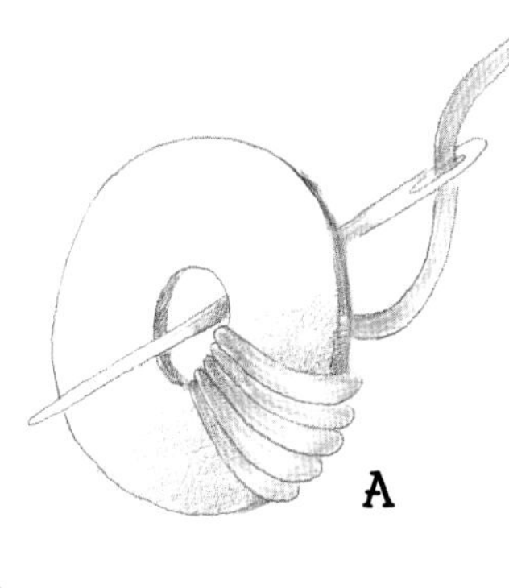

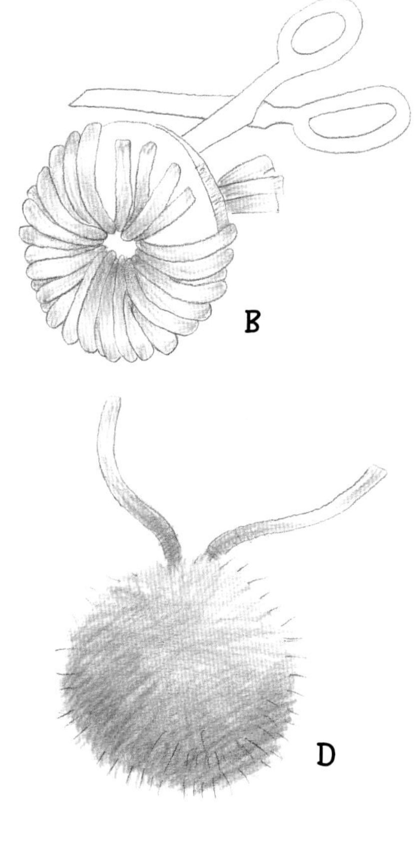

Making a Pompom

(Used for: Happy Elf Slippers, Cuddles the Clown Hat, Single Scoop Hat)

To make a pompom, cut two circles of cardboard, each equal to the size of the finished pompom, plus approximately ½ inch (1.3 cm), plus the diameter of the center hole. Holding the two circles together, cut a hole in the center, large enough to wind your yarn through. Wind the yarn through the holes in the center and around the edges until the hole is full (A).

Cut the yarn between the two circles (B). Wrap a double strand of yarn through the center and knot (C). Remove the cardboard and trim the pompom (D).

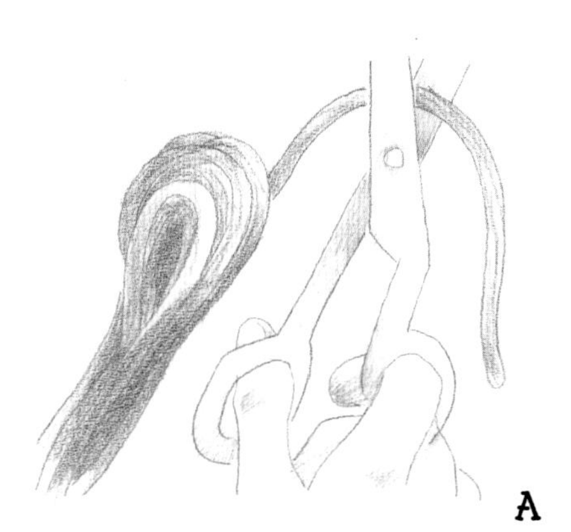

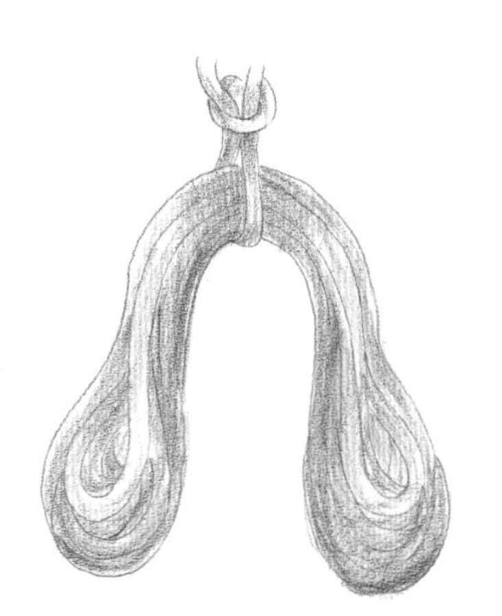

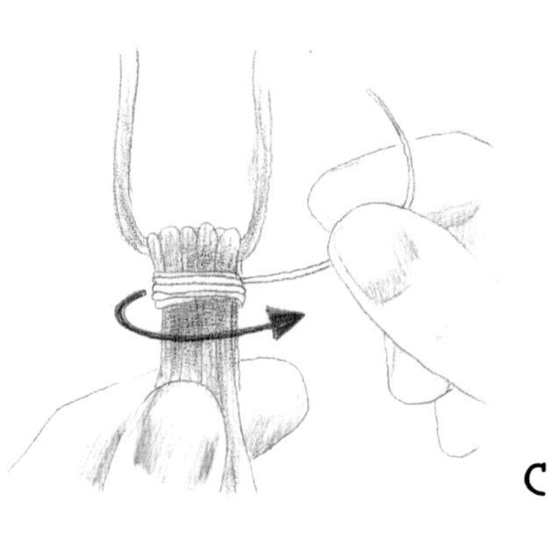

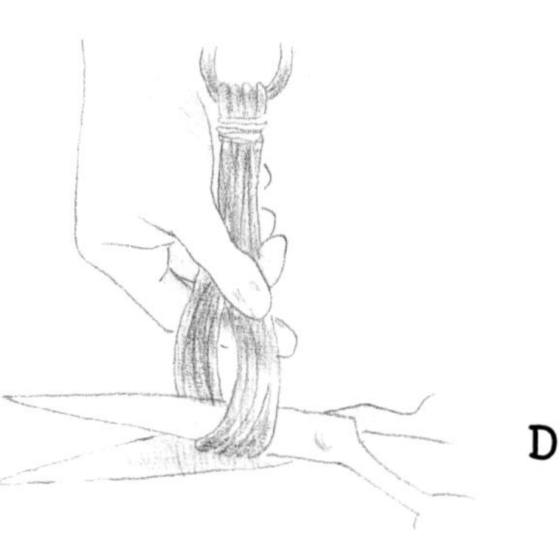

Making a Tassel

(Used for: Petite Prince or Princess Crown and Cape)

Cut a piece of cardboard the length you want your tassel to be. Wind a length of yarn several times around the cardboard. Remove the cardboard. Cut one strand for a tie (A). Wrap the tie tightly around the center of the bundle (B). Wrap a piece of yarn tightly a few times about 1 inch (2.5 cm) below the top of the folded bundle, securing ends with a knot (C). Cut the ends of the tassel (D).

YARN CONSIDERATIONS

Most of the projects in this book are made with cotton yarn. The colors available in cotton are usually very rich and saturated, even the pastels. Yarn companies create palettes to coordinate with each other, but you can still use unusual combinations in your work, such as violet and lime green, delft blue and pumpkin, etc.

The texture of cotton yarn is also very inviting. It's not scratchy like wool yarn and it's softer than acrylic—perfect for baby crochet projects. Using worsted weight (see page 25) cotton yarn reduces the time it takes to make a project, but you can also try using baby or fingering weight cotton yarn. It's thinner, so you'll need more stitches to create the same size hat.

Cotton yarn is easy to use, although it may take you a few minutes to get used to if you have been crocheting with wool or acrylic yarn—it doesn't bounce or stretch like those yarns do.

Another reason I chose cotton yarns is that they are readily available and affordable at craft, hobby, and discount stores. You can also easily find them online.

Cotton yarn is machine washable and can be dried in a dryer, with one caveat: remove the item from the dryer halfway through the cycle, shape it with your hands, and then let it air dry.

Yarn Weights

The weight of a yarn refers to its thickness. Here's a guide that you can refer to if you need to make yarn substitutions for some of the projects.

FINGERING WEIGHT: Loosely spun, very lightweight yarn used for delicate items.

SPORT WEIGHT: Medium-weight yarn.

WORSTED WEIGHT: Medium-weight yarn, very popular for knitted and crocheted items.

CHUNKY: Heavier than worsted weight, works up quickly.

BULKY: Very heavy, about twice the weight of worsted weight.

Checking Your Gauge

All patterns are based on a specific number of stitches and rows or round per inch (or metric equivalent). Checking your gauge is essential in order to ensure an accurate outcome for your pattern. To check your gauge, crochet a swatch with the yarn and needle/needles you intend to use. Your swatch should be at least 4 x 4 inches (10 x 10 cm) for a good sample. Check your row or stitch count in comparison to to the stated gauge for the project and adjust as necessary.

Projects

Make a hat or set that's as unique as the lovely little one in your life. Imagine your favorite toddler in a prince or princess crown and cape, or your beach-bound baby in a sailor's cap, or any of the other darling dress-up projects in the Whimsical Characters section of the book. The Garden Delights and Fresh Picks sections offer a creative take on nature's best: flowers, fruit and veggie hats and accessories, and even a little acorn hat. In the Lovable Zoo section, you'll find hats, mitts, and booties that transform a little one into a cuddly creature. And the Sweet Treats section is the icing on the cake: delightful confections that you'll find hard to resist. Whichever projects you choose, they're sure to please parents and little ones alike.

Whimsical Characters

Every day can be dress-up day with the witty and whimsical projects from this section of the book. Turn a tot into a happy elf with a pointy hat and slippers, or give your little cowboy or cowgirl a hat and boots to wear around the ranch. There's something for everyone in this darling collection.

Petite Prince or Princess Crown and Cape

Your favorite baby deserves a crown and cape fit for royalty. Feel free to add your own embellishments, such as the little monarch's name and title embroidered on the crown.

SKILL LEVEL
Intermediate

Size

HAT
20 inches (51 cm)

CAPE
8 inches (20.3 cm) long, adjustable neck

Stitches Used

single crochet (sc)
reverse single crochet (rc)
double crochet (dc)
half-double crochet (hdc)
increases (inc)
decreases (dec)
picot
back stitch
running stitch

Gauge

CROWN
3 stitches = 1 inch (2.5 cm)
3 rounds = 1 inch (2.5 cm)

CAPE
3 st = 1 inch (2.5 cm)
2 dc rounds = 1 inch (2.5 cm)

You Will Need

3 skeins (120 yds/109 m) worsted weight cotton yarn in grape

1 skein (120 yds/109 m) worsted weight cotton yarn in gold

1 skein (60 yds/54 m) fingering weight eyelash yarn in white

Yarn scraps in red and brown for embroidery

Size G crochet hook (for border, cord, and tassels)

Tapestry needle

Stitch markers

Purchased gold cord and tassels (optional)

CROWN

Body of Crown

ROUND 1: With grape, ch 6, join, ch 1, 15 sc in circle, join, ch 1. Place st marker here.

ROUND 2: 2 sc around. Join, ch 1.

ROUND 3: Sc around (30 st) (beg ch counts as 1 st), join, ch 1.

ROUND 4: *Inc, sc* repeat around, join, ch 1.

ROUND 5: Sc around, join, ch 1.

ROUND 6: *Inc, 2 sc,* repeat around, join, ch 1.

ROUNDS 7 TO 16 (OR LONGER IF DESIRED): Sc around, join and ch 1 at the end of each row.

Edging

Rc around bottom edge on back loop only. Fasten off.

Outer Rim of Crown

ROUND 1: Sl st gold yarn on where grape yarn is fastened off in front loop of last round. *Sc, hdc, 3 dc in one sp, hdc, sc, 5 sl st,* repeat around and begin to spiral.

ROUNDS 2 TO 7: Using back loops only, continue zigzag pattern by making 1 sc in each st, except at top of 3 dc: 3 sc, and on center bottom sl st, make a triple dec. You may spiral rounds 2 to 7, keeping track of each new round with a st marker.

ROUND 8: *Sl st up to a peak, 5-ch picot, 4 sl st to bottom of circle, 4 sl st, 2-ch picot, 4 sl st, 2-ch picot, 4 sl st*, around. Fasten off. Hide ends.

Embroidery

Using the front loops of sc as a guide, embroider the vine with brown in back stitch (see page 21), then embroider the red "jewels" onto the vine with running stitches (see page 20). If you like, choose different colors for the jewels on the crown, or embroider the baby's name: Queen Mira, King Josh, etc.

CAPE

ROW 1: With grape, ch 41. Starting in third ch from hk, *dc, 2 ch, sk 1 st* across row, ending on a dc, ch 3, turn.

ROW 2: Dc in same st as ch 1, *5 dc, 2 dc inc* repeat from *, working across the row, ending on a 2-dc inc, ch 3, turn.

ROW 3: Dc across, ch 3 and turn.

ROW 4: *2 dc inc, 6 dc* repeat around, ch 3 and turn.

ROW 5: Dc across, ch 3, and turn.

ROW 6: *Dc inc, 7 dc* across, ch 3 and turn.

ROW 7: Dc across, ch 3, and turn.

ROW 8: Dc inc, 8 dc, ch 3, and turn. Continue the pattern until 10 dc, or more for a longer cape. Make a ch 3 and turn at the end of each row except the last one.

NOTE: The pattern here is a row with no inc, then a row with inc, followed by same number of dc of previous inc row plus 1. Continue until desired length. Fasten off.

Fur Border

Still using the size G hk, attach the eyelash yarn to a corner of the cape, 3 sc in the corner. Along the sides of the dc rows, 2 sc for each dc, and sc around the cape, making corners with 3 sc. Go around the cape three times.

Cord

With soft gold, ch 6, sl st into first chain to form a loop. Ch about 130 (about 38 inches [96.5 cm]), go back 6 chs and sl st to form another loop. Sl st into each ch, all the way back to the beg loop. The loops will hold the tassels. Thread the cord through loops on neck of the cape.

Tassels

Use soft gold to make the tassels in the manner described on page 23 or use two purchased gold tassels and add them to the end of the cord.

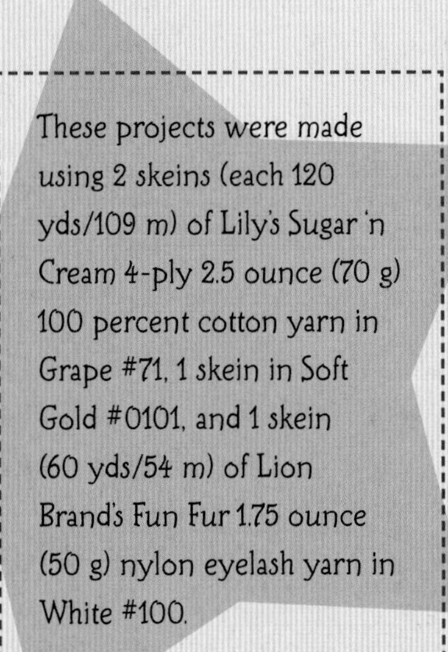

Happy Elf Hat and Slippers

Holiday time is picture time, and grandparents and relations of all kinds will adore a picture of their favorite toddler in this elf hat and slippers. The beard or chin strap is a wonderful detail that keeps the hat in place and keeps friends and relatives amused!

SKILL LEVEL

Intermediate

Size

HAT

21 to 22 inches (53.3 to 56 cm)

SLIPPERS

9- to 12-month size (see page 19)

Stitches Used

single crochet (sc)
half-double crochet (hdc)
increases (inc)
decreases (dec)

Gauge

3 st = 1 inch (2.5 cm)

You Will Need

3 skeins (each 120 yds/109 m) worsted weight cotton yarn in green

1 skein (60 yards/54 m) fingering weight eyelash yarn in white for chin strap (optional)

Size G crochet hook (for hat)

Size F crochet hook (for slippers)

2 small, clear or white buttons for beard/chinstrap (optional)

Tapestry needle

Purchased green pompoms (optional)

Stitch markers

Pattern Notes

The hat is a little off-center, so don't worry about mistakes. If you have too many or too few stitches, it only adds to the fun. There are notes in the directions for making both the hat and the slippers one size larger.

SLIPPER

(make two)

Start at tip of toe.

ROUND 1: With green and the size F hk, ch 3, sl st back 1, 5 sc in ch, join to first sc, ch 1. Place a st marker here and move it to the first st of every round from now on. Rounds will be worked in a spiral.

ROUND 2: *Inc, sc* twice, sc.

ROUND 3: 2 sc, hdc, 2 dc, hdc, sc.

ROUND 4: Sc, hdc, *inc using dc* twice, hdc, 3 sc.

ROUND 5: 2 sc, inc in next 4 st, 3 sc.

ROUND 6: 13 sc.

ROUND 7: 2 sc, *inc, 3 sc* 2 times, inc, 2 sc.

ROUND 8: Sc around (16 st).

ROUND 9: 2 sc, *inc, 4 sc* 2 times, inc, 3 sc.

ROUNDS 10 AND 11: Sc around for 2 rounds (do more rounds here if you would like longer slippers).

ROUND 12: 12 sc, ch 1.

ROUND 13: Turn work and sc back 10 st, ch 1.

ROUNDS 14 TO 20: 3 sc in first st, 7 sc, 3 sc in last st, ch 1.

ROUND 21: Snip off the yarn leaving a 12-inch (30.5 cm) tail. Thread this tail onto the tapestry needle. Hold the first and the last st of the round together, and sew down the back of the slipper with a whipstitch. Fasten off and fold the top of the back over so that it points down.

HAT

ROUND 1: Using green yarn and the size G hk, ch 4, join to first ch to form circle, ch 1, 7 sc in circle, join, place st marker to keep track of round beg, as this hat is made in a spiral.

ROUND 2: Starting in ch 1 st, sc around.

ROUND 3: Sc around.

ROUND 4: *Inc, 3 sc* twice (10 st).

ROUNDS 5 AND 6: Sc around.

ROUND 7: *Inc, 4 sc* twice.

ROUNDS 8 AND 9: Sc around.

ROUND 10: *Inc, 3 sc* 3 times.

ROUNDS 11 AND 12: Sc around.

ROUND 13: *Inc, 4 sc* 3 times.

ROUNDS 14 AND 15: Sc around.

ROUND 16: *Inc, 3 sc* 4 times, inc, sc.

ROUNDS 17 AND 18: Sc around.

ROUND 19: *Inc, 3 sc* 5 times, inc, 2 sc.

ROUNDS 20 AND 21: Sc around.

ROUND 22: *Inc, 4 sc* 5 times, inc, 3 sc.

ROUNDS 23 AND 24: Sc around.

ROUND 25: *Inc, 5 sc* 5 times, inc, 4 sc.

ROUNDS 26 AND 27: Sc around.

ROUND 28: *Inc, 5 sc * 6 times, inc, 4 sc.

ROUNDS 29 AND 30: Sc around.

ROUND 31: *Inc, 4 sc* 9 times, inc, 2 sc.

ROUNDS 32 AND 33: Sc around.

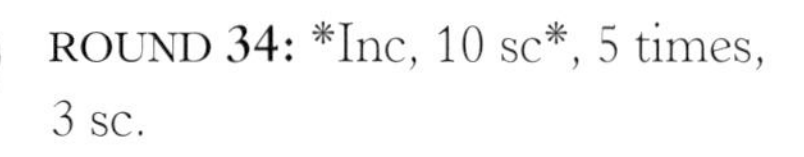

ROUND 34: *Inc, 10 sc*, 5 times, 3 sc.

NOTE: For a larger hat, you may increase the same amount, as in the pattern in Round 34, in Round 42.

ROUNDS 35 TO 41: Sc around.

Shaping the Bottom of the Hat

ROUND 42: 19 sc, 3 sc (shell) in one st (st marker), 23 sc across front of hat (st marker), 3 sc in one st, 19 sc, 3 sc in 1 st. 2 sl st and fasten off.

ROUND 43: The next two rounds will be on the back of the hat only. At second st marker, tie on the yarn to preceding sc, sl st, 3 sc in one st (over last shell), 22 sc, 3 sc in one st (over last shell), 20 sc, 3 sc, sl st, fasten off.

ROUND 44: Repeat shaping of last round: Starting on the left side of the face, join yarn, sl st, sc, 3 sc in one st over last shell, 24 sc, 3 sc in 1 st over previous shell, 23 sc, 3 sc in one st, sc, sl st, fasten off.

ROUND 45: Repeat shaping, starting at the left side of the face, shells over previous shells, etc., but do not fasten off.

ROUND 46: Sc around the face and the back of the hat, 2 sl st, and fasten off.

Make (see page 22) or purchase three green pompoms and add to tip of hat and insteps of slippers.

Detachable Beard or Chin Strap

ROUND 1: With the F hk and white, leave a 4-inch (10 cm) tail, ch 5, in second ch from hk, make a round of 4 sc, ch 1, and turn.

ROUNDS 2 TO 38: 4 sc, ch 1 for about 10-inches (25.4 cm) or to size of the child. Fasten off leaving a 4-inch tail (10 cm). Attach small buttons to the ends of the chin strap and button into an available hole in the crocheted sideburns of the hat.

This project was made using 3 skeins (120 yds/109 m) each of Lily's Sugar 'n Cream 4-ply 2.5 ounce (70 g) 100 percent cotton yarn in Green #062, and 1 skein (60 yds/54 m) of Lion Brand's Fun Fur 1.75 ounce (50 g) nylon eyelash yarn in White #100.

Ahoy Matey! Hat

A handsome hat for your little first mate, this simple pattern is dressed up a bit with some easy embroidery stitches on the cuff.

SKILL LEVEL
Beginner

Size

22 inches (56 cm)

Stitches Used

single crochet (sc)
running stitch

Gauge

3 stitches =1 inch (2.5 cm)

You Will Need

1 skein (120 yds/109 m) worsted weight cotton yarn in white

Size F crochet hook

Cotton yarns in red, yellow, and blue for embroidery

Dressmaker's chalk

Tapestry needle

Stitch markers

HAT

ROUND 1: Starting at top of the hat, ch 5, join to first ch to make circle, ch 1, 12 sc in circle, join, mark the beg of ea round (the hat is made in a spiral), ch 1.

ROUND 2: 2 sc in ea st around.

ROUND 3: Sc around.

ROUND 4: *Inc, sc* around.

ROUND 5: Sc around.

ROUND 6: *Inc, 2 sc* around.

ROUND 7: Sc around.

ROUND 8: *Inc, 3 sc* around.

ROUND 9: Sc around.

ROUND 10: *Inc, 4 sc* around.

ROUNDS 11 TO 25: Sc around. At then end of round 25, make 2 sl sts.

ROUNDS 26 TO 34: To make the hat cuff, turn the hat so the opening is facing you, sc in top loop for first round only, then continue to spiral in both loops.

ROUND 35: Inc, 23 sc, inc, 23 sc, inc, 23 sc.

ROUNDS 36 TO 38: Sc around.

ROUND 39: Inc, 17 sc, inc, 17 sc, inc, 17 sc, inc, 19 sc, fasten off.

Embroidery

Find the center of the cuff (third round front) and mark. Thread 2 feet (61 cm) of red yarn onto the tapestry needle. Make the boat outline by making a 2-inch (2.5 cm) line with two running stitches (see page 20) in red across the center of the mark on the third round. Go up the front of the boat, across the top of the boat, down the back of the boat, then make the mast and sails. Fasten off red. Thread 1 foot (30.5 cm) of yellow on the needle and make the flag on the top of the mast, and a few stripes on the sails. Fasten off. Thread 2 feet (61 cm) of blue yarn to make zigzag waves under the boat. Fasten off. Hide all ends.

This project was made using 1 skein (120 yds/109 m) of Lily's Sugar 'n Cream 4-ply 2.5 ounce (70 g) 100 percent cotton yarn in White #001.

Swiss Miss Hat

This imaginative hat is sure to elicit a smile (or even a chuckle) from everyone who sees it. If the braids are just too much for you, you can make the hat without them. If you do choose to use braids, secure them tightly to the hat—little hands love to tug on them!

SKILL LEVEL

Intermediate

Size

22 inches (55.8 cm)
19 inches (48.3 cm) (see note below Round 15)

Stitches Used

single crochet (sc)
reverse single crochet (rc)
increases (inc)
embroidery stitches
Algerian eyelet stitch
daisy stitch
running stitch

Gauge

3 st = 1 inch (2.5 cm)

You Will Need

2 skeins (each 120 yds/109 m) worsted weight cotton yarn in forest green

1 skein (120 yds/109 m) worsted weight cotton yarn in yellow

Embroidery yarn scraps in red, light green, and white

Size G crochet hook

Stitch markers

Tapestry needle

Dressmaker's chalk

Scissors

Cardboard or mat board

Pattern Notes

This is a very warm hat because of the double cuff. You may embroider something else on the cuff, too—a name, initials, animals, etc.

HAT

ROUND 1: Ch 5, join to form circle, ch 1, 8 sc in circle. Place st marker to remember beg of rounds. The hat is crocheted in a spiral.

ROUND 2: 2 sc in each st.

ROUNDS 3 AND 4: Sc around.

ROUND 5: *Inc, sc* 8 times around.

ROUNDS 6 AND 7: Sc around.

ROUND 8: *Inc, 2 sc* 8 times around.

ROUNDS 9 AND 10: Sc around.

ROUND 11: *Inc, 3 sc* around.

ROUND 12: Sc around.

ROUND 13: *Inc, 4 sc* around.

ROUND 14: Sc around.

ROUND 15: *Inc, 2 sc* around.

NOTE: To make a smaller hat, make 3 sc here instead of 2 sc. This will result in a hat that is about 19 inches [48.3 cm] in diameter.

ROUNDS 16 TO 29: Sc around in a spiral, and make one sl st at the end of round 29.

ROUND 30: Turn the hat around so the opening is facing you and, working in top loop only, continue to sc around to form the cuff.

ROUNDS 31 TO 42: Continue to spiral around the hat in sc. 1 sl st on the last st.

ROUND 43: Rc around. Fasten off.

Embroidery

On the front of the hat, find the top of Round 6 and mark that st sp. Lightly mark about 3 inches (7.6 cm) on either side of that sp with dressmaker's chalk. Thread the yellow yarn onto the tapestry needle and make the Algerian eyelet stitch (see page 21) around the center space for the middle flower. Tie off. With dressmaker's chalk, mark quarters of this circle (flower center) and then eighths. Thread the red yarn and make eight daisy stitches (see page 20) at marks. Tie off. Mark with chalk for edelweiss flowers and branch. Embroider with running stitch and daisy stitch (see page 20).

Optional Braid (make two)

Wind a piece of yellow yarn 50 times around a stiff 7-inch (17.8 cm) long piece of cardboard or mat board. Cut two 10-inch (25.4 cm) pieces of yellow yarn, slip one through the loops, and tie it around one end of wound yarn. This tie will also bind the braid to the hat. Snip the opposite end of the yarn bundle off the cardboard. Smooth down the yellow yarn, and then divide it into three sections to braid. You may tie the yarn bundle to something in order to braid it, or just braid on a surface, smoothing the yarn as you go. At the end of the braid, tie with the other 10-inch (25.4 cm) piece of yarn and hide ends. Trim the end of the braid even. Two 10-inch (25.4 cm) pieces of red yarn may be cut and tied to the ends of the braids in little bows.

Tying on Braids

Find the second to last round of crochet inside the hat above the bottom round of loops. At approximately the same width apart as the embroidery, tie on braids. Hide ends.

This project was made using 2 skeins (each 120 yds/ 109 m) of Lily's Sugar 'n Cream 4-ply 2.5 ounce (70 g) 100 percent cotton yarn in Dark Pine #016 and 1 skein in Yellow #010.

Cuddles the Clown Hat & Ruff

For a birthday or a day at the circus, you can't beat the cute factor in this hat and ruff set. It's easy enough for a beginner to make.

SKILL LEVEL
Beginner

Size

HAT
At least 15½ inches (39.4 cm) (sits on top of head rather than stretching around head)

SMALL RUFF
Approximately 6 inches (15 cm)

LARGE RUFF
Approximately 7 inches (17.8 cm)

Stitches Used

single crochet (sc)
increases (inc)

Gauge

4 stitches = 1 inch (2.5 cm)
4 rounds = 1 inch (2.5 cm)

You Will Need

1 skein (120 yds/109 m) worsted weight cotton yarn in each of the following colors: pumpkin, yellow, delft blue, white (for ruff)

Size E crochet hook

Scissors

Purchased pompoms (optional)

1-inch (2.5 cm) wide satin ribbon for bow tie, approximately 19 inches (48.3 cm)

Pattern Notes

Orange and yellow alternate, 7 rounds each, down the hat.

HAT

ROUND 1: With yellow, ch 5, join to first ch to form circle, ch 1, 12 sc in circle, join to first ch, ch 1.

ROUND 2: Sc around (12 sc), join, ch 1.

ROUND 3: *5 sc, inc* 2 times, join, ch 1.

ROUND 4: 14 sc around, join, ch 1.

ROUND 5: 4 sc, inc, 4 sc, inc, 3 sc, inc, join, ch 1.

ROUND 6: 17 sc around, join, ch 1.

ROUND 7: 5 sc, inc, 5 sc, inc, 4 sc, inc, join with orange yarn, ch 1.

ROUND 8: Continuing with orange, 20 sc, join, ch 1.

ROUND 9: 6 sc, inc, 6 sc, inc, 5 sc, inc, join, ch 1.

ROUND 10: 23 sc around, join, ch 1.

ROUND 11: 7 sc, inc, 7 sc, inc, 6 sc, inc, join, ch 1.

ROUND 12: 26 sc around, join, ch 1.

ROUND 13: 8 sc, inc, 8 sc, inc, 7 sc, inc, join, ch 1.

ROUND 14: 29 sc around, join with yellow, ch 1.

ROUND 15: Continuing with yellow, 9 sc, inc, 9 sc, inc, 8 sc, inc, join, ch 1.

ROUND 16: 32 sc around, join, ch 1.

ROUND 17: 10 sc, inc, 10 sc, inc, 9 sc, inc, join, ch 1.

ROUND 18: 35 sc around, join, ch 1.

ROUND 19: 11 sc, inc, 11 sc, inc, 10 sc, inc, join, ch 1.

ROUND 20: 38 sc around, join, ch 1.

ROUND 21: 12 sc, inc, 12 sc, inc, 11 sc, inc, join with orange, ch 1.

ROUND 22: 41 sc around, join, ch 1.

ROUND 23: 13 sc, inc, 13 sc, inc, 12 sc, inc, join, ch 1.

ROUND 24: 44 sc around, join, ch 1.

ROUND 25: 14 sc, inc, 14 sc, inc, 13 sc, inc, join, ch 1.

ROUND 26: 47 sc around, join, ch 1.

ROUND 27: 15 sc, inc, 15 sc, inc, 14 sc, inc, join, ch 1.

ROUND 28: 50 sc around, join with yellow, ch 1.

ROUND 29: 16 sc, inc, 16 sc, inc, 15 sc, inc, join, ch 1.

ROUND 30: 53 sc around, join, ch 1.

ROUND 31: 17 sc, inc, 17 sc, inc, 16 sc, inc, join, ch 1.

ROUND 32: 56 sc around, join, ch 1.

ROUND 33: 18 sc, inc, 18 sc, inc, 17 sc, inc, join, ch 1.

ROUND 34: 59 sc around, join, ch 1.

ROUND 35: 19 sc, inc, 19 sc, inc, 18 sc, inc, join with orange, ch 1.

ROUND 36: 62 sc around, join, ch 1.

NOTE: For a 15 ½ inch (43.2 cm) hat, make two more rounds of 62 sc, then fasten off. For larger sizes, add a seven-round color section for each additional 1 inch (2.5 cm).

Hat Brim Ruffle

ROUND 1: Tie on blue yarn, 3 sc in each st around the bottom of the hat, top loop only, around, join, ch 1.

ROUND 2: Sc around, join. Fasten off. Arrange ruffles.

Pompom (make four)

See the instructions for making pompoms on page 22. Fluff the pompom by flicking it on the edge of the table. Trim the pompoms to an even, tight shape. Tie the first one onto the hat top, and the remaining three onto the hat front, centering them on three stripes.

Neck Strap

There are two ways to make a neck strap.

OPTION 1: Cut a 1-foot (91.4 cm) strip of elastic and tie it to opposite inside edges of the hat.

OPTION 2: Leaving a 6-inch (15 cm) tail of yarn, ch 80, starting in second ch from hk, sl st all the way back to the end, fasten off and leave a 6-inch (15 cm) tail of yarn. Use the tails to fasten the ties to the lower rim of the hat on either side.

SMALL RUFF

ROUND 1: Ch 6 and join to first ch to form loop for the ribbon. Ch 36, join the last ch to the sixth from last st to form another loop. Ch 1 and 3 sc in each ch down length, stopping at the loop.

ROUNDS 2 TO 6: Sc around, ch 1 at end of each round to turn. Fasten off after the seventh round.

LARGE RUFF

ROUND 1: Ch 6, join to form loop, ch 46, go back 6 st, sl st to form loop. Ch 1 and 4 sc in each ch. Ch 1.

ROUNDS 2 TO 6: Sc around, ch 1. Fasten off.

NOTE: The ruff can be made any size by adding to or subtracting from the original chain.

This project was made with 1 skein (120 yds/109 m) each of Lily's Sugar 'n Cream 4-ply 2.5 ounce (70 g) 100 percent cotton yarn in Pumpkin #1132, Delft Blue #28, and Yellow #10.

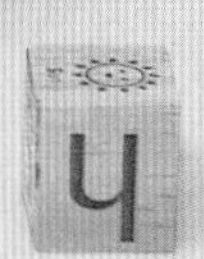

Baby Artist Beret

Your baby artist can step out in style with this sized-to-fit traditional beret. Make yourself a matching one by following the pattern notes.

SKILL LEVEL
Intermediate

Size

19 inches (48.3 cm)

Stitches Used

single crochet (sc)
increases (inc)
decreases (dec)
spiraling

Gauge

4 st = 1 inch (2.5 cm)

You Will Need

2 skeins (each 105 yds/96 m) sportweight alpaca yarn in black

Size F crochet hook

Stitch markers

HAT

FOUNDATION: Ch 5, beg in second ch from hk, sl st to bottom, to form a tab at the center.

ROUND 1: Ch 5 and join to form circle. Ch 1, 12 sc in circle, join, ch 1.

ROUND 2: 2 sc around. The hat is made in a spiral, so place a marker at the end of each round.

ROUND 3: Sc around.

ROUND 4: *Inc, sc* around.

ROUND 5: Sc around.

ROUND 6: *Inc, 2 sc* around.

ROUND 7: Sc around.

ROUND 8: *Inc, 3 sc* around.

ROUND 9: Sc around.

ROUND 10: *Inc, 4 sc* around.

ROUND 11: Sc around.

ROUND 12: *Inc, 5 sc* around.

ROUND 13: Sc around.

ROUND 14: *Inc, 6 sc* around.

ROUND 15: Sc around.

ROUND 16: *Inc, 7 sc* around.

ROUND 17: Sc around.

ROUND 18: *Inc, 8 sc* around.

ROUND 19: Sc around.

NOTE: As you can see, there is a pattern of increases to make the circle top of the beret. The pattern is: 1 round of sc in each st, then a round of regular inc, with one more st in sc. At this point, the pattern can be further increased to make an adult beret (you'll need more yarn, of course), or fewer rows of inc will make a very small beret. The underside of the beret has dec in the same pattern for the opening, and these are also adjustable.

ROUND 20: *Dec, 8 sc* around.

ROUND 21: Sc around.

Continue to decrease in the pattern until the desired head size is reached or there are only 3 st between decs. Make the last round a non-dec round, then make one sl st and fasten off. Hide ends.

This project was made with 2 skeins (each 105 yds/96 m) of Australian Heirloom's 8-ply 1.75 ounce (50 g) alpaca yarn in Black #985.

Little Wrangler Hat and Boots

For riding the open range or just riding around in the stroller, this set is sure to please the little cowboys and cowgirls and their parents, too.

SKILL LEVEL
Beginner to Intermediate

Size

HAT
23 inches (55.8 cm)

BOOTS
12- to 36-month size (see page 19)

Stitches Used

single crochet (sc)
double crochet (dc)
half-double crochet (hdc)
triple crochet (tr)
increases (inc)
decreases (dec)
picot
whipstitch
running stitch

Gauge

3 stitches = 1 inch (2.5 cm)

You Will Need

3 skeins (each 236 yds/212 m) of worsted weight cotton yarn in red

1 skein (115 yds/105 m) worsted weight metallic yarn in silver

1 skein (120 yds/109 m) worsted weight cotton yarn in white

1 skein (120 yds/109 m) worsted weight cotton yarn in black

Hairclips or safety pins to hold pieces together while joining

Size F crochet hook

Size E crochet hook

Wooden bead with large hole for hat tie

Tapestry needle

HAT

(starting at crown)

ROUND 1: With red and size F hk, ch 11, in second ch from hk, 7 sc down chain, 5 sc in end space, sc 7 down other side of chain. 5 sc in end space with first ch. You may place a contrasting piece of yarn or a st marker here to remember where the rounds begin and end as spiraling begins here.

ROUND 2: 7 sc, 5 inc around the 5 end sts, 7 sc, 5 inc.

ROUND 3: Sc around (34 sts).

ROUND 4: 8 sc, *inc, sc* 5 times, 7 sc, *inc, sc* 5 times.

ROUND 5: Sc around (44 sts).

ROUND 6: 8 sc *inc, 2 sc*, 5 times, 9 sc, *inc, 2 sc* 5 times.

ROUND 7: Sc around (54 sts).

ROUND 8: 9 sc, *inc, 3 sc* 5 times, 7 sc, *inc, 3 sc* 5 times.

ROUND 9: Sc around (64 sts).

ROUND 10: 8 sc, *inc, 4 sc* 5 times, 7 sc, *inc, 4 sc* 5 times.

ROUND 11: Sc around.

ROUND 12: In top loop only (this forms the fold between the crown of the hat and the sides), sc around.

ROUNDS 13 TO 25: Spiral sc in each st around, in both loops.

ROUND 26: Begin hat brim: In top loop only, *inc, 2 sc* around.

ROUNDS 27 TO 30: Sc around.

ROUND 31: Begin inc in front and back of brim: 16 sc, inc, 47 sc, inc, finish round in sc.

ROUND 32: Sc around.

ROUND 33: 10 sc, *inc, 3 sc* 5 times, 29 sc, *inc, 3 sc* 5 times, finish round in sc.

ROUND 34: Sc around.

ROUND 35: 9 sc, *inc, 4 sc* 5 times, 29 sc, *inc, 4 sc* 5 times, finish round with sc.

ROUND 36: Sc around, end with 2 sl st. Fasten off.

EDGE OF BRIM: Cut 5 feet (1.5 m) each of black and white cotton yarn, and thread both on the tapestry needle. Whipstitch (see page 21) along the last row of the brim, every 3 sts with the double yarns. Fasten off.

Hat Tie

Cut 7 feet (2 m) each of the white and black yarns and tie together at one end. Tie one free end to a chair, and tie the other to a pencil. Stand about 14 feet (4 m) away, holding the pencil. Twist the pencil until there is enough twist in the half black/half white length of yarn to twist back on itself a little. Take the center knot and let the black and white strands intertwine. Wrap once around the bottom of the hat crown and push through holes in the crochet on the sides, using a crochet hk to pull the tie through. Use a wooden bead as a slide, and knot the ends of the ties.

BOOTS

Sole (make two)

ROW 1: With red, ch 2, turn; in first ch, 3 sc, ch 1, turn.

ROWS 2 TO 19: 3 sc; in last one, inc, ch 1, turn. Continue working rows in sc with inc at end for a total of 7 sc. Continue working 7 sc across rows for 14 rows and a total of 19 rows. Do not ch 1. Turn.

ROW 20: Sk first st, sl st second st, and 4 sc, sl st last st. Ch 1.

Without breaking off the yarn, continue to sc down side of the sole, doing one sc at the end of each row, 18 sc. At the very end of the toe, do an inc of 3 in the middle st of the first row to make a point. Continue down the other side with 1 sc in each row, 18 sc, sl st last st. Fasten off.

Boot Top (make four)

TIP: Leaving tails of yarn to be used later for sewing pieces together eliminates bulkiness and knots.

NOTE: See note on page 18 for an explanation of shells.

ROW 1: With red, leave a 2-foot (61 cm) tail on two of tops (for sewing tog later), ch 14, turn, 13 sc across, ch 1, turn, and repeat for a total of 8 rows. Ch 2.

ROW 2: Sc in second st from hk, sc across (14 sts). Repeat for seven more rows of 14 sts, ch 1, turn.

ROW 3: 4 sc, sk 2 st, 5 dc in next space (a shell), sk 2 st, 5 sc, ch 1, turn.

ROW 4: Sk first st, 1 sl st, sc, hdc, 3 dc, 3 dc in same sp, 2 dc, hdc, 2 sc, sl st.

Leave 1 foot (30.4 cm) of yarn on one of the sides of each pair and fasten off. Thread the extra yarn onto the tapestry needle and sew two boot tops tog along front seam down to inc only, and fasten off. Be sure to match up the sides so that the inc edges are tog at the front of the boot. Do both boots. Don't do back seams yet.

Toe Top (make two)

ROW 1: With red, ch 2, 3 sc in first ch, ch 1, turn.

ROW 2: Sc inc in first st, sc, inc in last st. Continue doing rows with inc in first and last sts until there are 11 sc across. Ch 1, turn.

ROW 3: 4 rows of sc with inc in first st only. Ch 1, turn.

ROW 4: On top loop of st only: Sk first st, 1 sl st, sc, hdc, 3 dc, 5 tr in 1 st, 3 dc, hdc, sc, 2 sl st.

ROW 5: Fasten off, leaving a 1-foot (30.4 cm) tail of yarn on both toe tops.

Bootstrap (make four)

With red yarn, ch 27, starting on second ch from hk, sc 26. Fasten off, leaving 1-foot (30.4 cm) tail. Line up the strap in the middle of the shell st at the top of the boot side (the edge without a tail should be at the bottom). Fold over the top of the strap at top of the boot to make a loop. You may pin the strap in place. The tail of yarn should be inside the boot. Thread the tail with the tapestry needle and loosely sew straight down boot strap, securing it to boot at bottom edge. Use black and white yarns threaded on the tapestry needle and whipstitch down the sides of the bootstraps.

Assembly and Embroidery of Boots

TIP: Tiny hair clips that look like toothed jaws are useful for clipping crochet pieces together while sewing.

Sew the toe tops to the boot tops, with the 5-tr shell at the top, matching rows, up one side and down the other. Toe tops should have ridges where only top loops were used.

Embroider S-curves, initials, or any favorite designs on the boot tops and toes with the black and white yarns.

Sew down the back seam on the boot tops (be sure bootstraps and embroidery are sewed on first). Use about 3 feet (91 cm) of red yarn to join the completed boot tops to the soles.

Optional Detachable Silver Spur (make two)

With silver and a size E hk, ch 5, join last ch to first chain to form circle. *Ch 3, sl st in second ch from hk, sc in 3rd ch, sl to circle* repeat around circle for 5 points of star/spur. Ch 52 and join to star near center. Fasten off, hide ends.

These projects were made using 3 skeins (each 236 yds/212m) of Lion Brand's Kitchen Cotton 4-ply 5 ounce (140 g) 100 percent cotton yarn in Poppy Red #112, 1 skein (120 yds/109 m) each of Lily's Sugar 'n Cream 4-ply 2.5 ounce (70 g) 100 percent cotton yarn in Black #002 and White #001, and 1 skein (115 yds/105 m) of Lion Brand's Glitterspun 1.75 ounce (50 g) acrylic yarn in Silver #150.

Sou'easter Hat and Boots

Bring on the grey skies and drizzle! Wearing this cheerful hat and boot set, your little one will add a dash of color to even the dreariest days.

SKILL LEVEL
Beginner

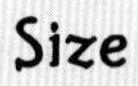

Size

HAT
18 inches (48 cm)

BOOTS
6-to 9-month size (see page 19)

Stitches Used

single crochet (sc)
half-double crochet (hdc)
increases (inc)

Gauge

3 stitches = 1 inch (2.5 cm)

You Will Need

1 skein (452 yds/413 m) worsted weight acrylic yarn in bright yellow

Size E crochet hook

Stitch marker

Tapestry needle

HAT

ROUND 1: Ch 5, join to first st to form circle, ch 1, 12 sc in circle, join, ch 1.

ROUND 2: 2 sc in ea st around, ch 1.

ROUND 3: Sc around, ch 1.

ROUND 4: *Inc, sc* around, ch 1.

ROUND 5: Sc around, ch 1.

ROUND 6: *Inc, 2 sc*, ch 1.

ROUND 7: Sc around, ch 1.

ROUND 8: *Inc, 3 sc*, ch 1.

ROUNDS 9 TO 23: Sc around. Ch 1 at the end of each round, except for last round, then join and ch 1.

ROUND 24 (TO START BRIM): On top loop for this round only make: *Inc, 8 sc* around, finish the round in sc, join, ch 3.

ROUND 25: 3 dc, 4 hdc, 50 sc, 4 hdc, 4 dc, join, ch 1.

ROUND 26: *Inc, 9 sc* around, finish round in sc, join and ch 3.

ROUND 27: 9 dc, 4 hdc, 45 sc, 4 hdc, 10 dc, join, ch 1.

ROUND 28: *Inc, 10 sc* around, finish round in sc, join, ch 3.

ROUND 29: 12 dc, 4 hdc, 47 sc, 4 hdc, 13 dc, join, ch 1.

ROUND 30: *Inc, 11 sc*, finish the round in sc, join, ch 3.

ROUND 31: 16 dc, 4 hdc, 47 sc, 4 hdc, 17 dc, join, ch 1.

ROUND 32: *Inc, 12 sc*, finish round in sc, join, fasten off.

ROUND 33: Sl st around, join, and fasten off.

BOOTS

Sole (make two)

Start at toe end.

ROW 1: Ch 6, starting in second ch from hk, 5 sc, ch 1, turn.

ROW 2: 4 sc, inc in last st of row, ch 1, turn.

ROW 3: 5 sc, inc in last st of row, ch 1, turn.

ROWS 4 TO 15: 7 sc across, ch 1, turn.

ROW 16: Sk first st, 6 sc, ch 1, turn.

ROW 17: Sk first st, 5 sc, ch 1.

ROW 18: Make a row of sts outlining sole: Starting at second to last row, sc at the end of every row down side of sole, at toe corners 3 sc, go down other side of sole but do not go across heel, ch 1, turn work.

Sides of Upper Boot

Going back over the outline just made, work sc into the top loop of stitches all the way around, including the heel. At the end of the row, join to the first ch and ch 1. Make two more rows around the sides, still using top loops of st. Fasten off.

Toe Tops (make two)

ROW 1: Ch 2, in second ch from hk, 5 sc, ch 1, turn.

ROW 2: 2 sc in ea st across, ch 1, turn.

ROW 3: Sc across, ch 1, turn.

ROW 4: *Inc, sc* across, ch 2, do not turn.

ROW 5: Going across bottom of toe top just made, 8 sc, ch 1, turn.

ROWS 6 AND 7: 9 sc across (1 st will be from previous row).

Measure a 12-inch (30.5 cm) tail of yarn, snip and fasten off. Use the tail of the yarn to sew on the toe top, centering on the toe of the boot. Fasten off.

Top

Tie the yarn on the right side toe piece at last st above sides. For this part it's easier to spiral than join rounds, so place a row marker here.

ROUND 1: Sc around top of shoe, in back loop only, around the top of sides and sl st loosely across toe piece.

ROUND 2: Hdc in corner where toe meets top, continue to sc around, working in both loops. When you get to the toe top, hdc in corner st, sc across the toe piece in the back loop.

ROUNDS 3 TO 16: Sc around opening, up the height of the boot.

ROUND 17: Sl st loosely around the boot top, fasten off.

This project was made using 1 skein (452 yds/413 m) of Coats and Clark's Red Heart Supersaver 4-ply 8 ounce (226 g) acrylic yarn in Bright Yellow #2120.

Garden Delights

Make one of these
blooming beauties for
your little flower girl, or
celebrate fall with a darling
acorn cap. These fun
and functional projects
are the ones parents will
"pick" everyday.

Rose Fairy Hat

With its delicate design and color, this darling hat transforms a little girl into a flower fairy. This project is a little more complicated than some of the others, but you'll have no trouble once you get the rhythm of the pattern.

SKILL LEVEL
Advanced

Size

20 inches (51 cm)

Stitches Used

single crochet (sc)
half-double crochet (hdc)
double crochet (dc)
triple crochet (tr)
picot stitch
increases (inc)
decreases (dec)

Gauge

3 st = 1 inch (2.5 cm)

You Will Need

2 skeins (each 120 yds/109 m) worsted weight cotton yarn in pink

1 skein (120 yds/109 m) worsted weight cotton yarn in green

Size F crochet hook

Pattern Notes

The hat is made in three steps. First, make the stem and thorns, then continue on down in rows for the calyx, which is the round green part at the base of a flower head. Next, make the sepals, the wing-shaped green things that stick out of the calyx. The sepals are each made separately, along a long chain, then joined to the base with 2 sl st, which is the green round calyx you made previously. Finally, you make the pink petal base and the petals.

Stem, Sepals, and Calyx

ROUND **1:** Starting with green for the stem, thorns, and first round of the hat, ch 12. Starting in second ch from hk, 3 sl st, 1-ch picot, 4 sl st, 1-ch picot, 3 sl st. In last ch, 8 sc, join to beg sc, ch 1.

ROUND **2:** Beg making the calyx: *Inc, 2 sc* around, join, ch 1.

ROUND **3:** Sc around, join, ch 1.

ROUND **4:** *Inc, 2 sc* around, join, ch 1.

ROUND **5:** Sc around, join, ch 1.

ROUND **6:** *Dec, 2 sc* repeat, join, ch 1.

ROUND **7:** Sc around, join, ch 1.

ROUND **8:** Working in front loop only, inc in each st around, join, ch 1.

ROUND **9:** Make sepals: *Ch 10, starting in second ch from hook, 5 sl st down chain, sc, hdc, dc, tr, skip 3 st in the base of the calyx, and make 2 sl st in the base* repeat to make 5 sepals, fasten off.

Petal Base

ROUND 1: With pink, attach yarn with sl st to a loop underneath Round 8. *Ch 4, sk 3 st, sl st into fourth st* repeat 2 more times, making three large loops. (Work from the inside of the hat).

ROUND 2: Ch 8, *dc in loop, ch 5, dc in sl st, ch 5* around. Sl st into third ch at beg of round to end round (this will make six large loops).

ROUND 3: Ch 8, dc in same sp, ch 4, *dc in next dc, ch 4, dc in same dc, ch 4* repeat in each dc around. Sl st into third ch at beg of round (12 loops).

ROUNDS 4 TO 9: Ch 8, *in next dc, ch 5*, around. Sl st into third ch at beg of round. At the end of Round 9, do not cut off yarn; turn work so that the hat top is facing you.

Petals

ROUND 1: With pink, in next loop, ch 1, *sc, hdc, 3 dc, hdc, sc*, repeat in all loops, around. Ch 4.

ROUNDS 2 TO 8: Go down to next loop below and to the left: *Sc, hdc, dc, 3 tr, dc, hdc, sc* in each of the 12 loops of this round. Ch 4 at the end of each round.

ROUND 9: On the first round of loops, near sepals, split the petals in half and do half a petal in each loop as follows: *Sc, hdc, dc, tr, in next part of loop is tr, dc, hdc, sc.* Repeat for 3 petals.

Fasten off. Hide ends.

This project was made using 2 skeins (120 yds/109 g) each of Lily's Sugar 'n Cream 4-ply 2.5 ounce (70 g) 100 percent cotton yarn in Sage Green #084 and Rose Pink #046.

Darling Daisy Hat and Purse

Petal power for your toddler! Parents love the sun coverage of the hat, and little girls love their own special purse for storing treats and treasures.

SKILL LEVEL

Beginner

Size

19 to 20 inches (48.3 to 50.8 cm)

Stitches Used

single crochet (sc)
double crochet (dc)
half-double crochet (hdc)
triple crochet (tr)
increases (inc)
picot stitch

Gauge

4 st = 1 inch (2.5 cm)

You Will Need

2 skeins (each 120 yds/109 m) worsted weight cotton yarn in light yellow

1 skein (120 yds/109 m) worsted weight cotton yarn in white

1 skein (120 yds/109 m) worsted weight cotton yarn in green (for the purse handle)

Size E crochet hook

Tapestry needle

Stitch markers

Pattern Notes

This hat is made in the sweater stitch (1 sc, 1 ch), which makes it stretchy. Sts are worked in chain spaces only. The hat is made in a spiral, so rounds should be marked (see Round 7).

See note on page 18 for an explanation of shells (Round 1 of petals).

HAT

(starting at top)

ROUND 1: With yellow, ch 5, join to form circle, ch 2, in circle make 11 sc, join, ch 2.

ROUND 2: *Sc, ch 1* around, join, ch 2. Crochet only into ch-1 sps from now on.

ROUND 3: *Sc, ch 1, twice in each ch-1 sp* (this will be called an inc) (12 sets of inc, including ch 2), (join, ch 2), ch 2.

ROUND 4: *Sc, ch 1* in each ch 1 sp, join, ch 2.

ROUND 5: *Inc, then sc, ch 1 in the next 2 ch-1 sp* around, join, ch 2.

ROUND 6: *Sc, ch 1 in each ch-1sp around*, join, ch 2.

ROUND 7: *Inc, then sc, ch 1 in the next 3 ch sp* repeat around, join, ch 2, place a st marker here.

ROUNDS 8 TO 23: *Sc, ch 1* in ea ch-1 sp spiral around hat (without joining), fasten off.

Petals

ROUND 1: Tie on white yarn at rim of hat and using back loop only, *1 sl st, 6 tr in fifth st from sl st, 2-ch picot, 5 more tr in same sp (shell), sk 4 st* and repeat around.

ROUND 2: 1 sl st. Using front loop spaces from Round 1, *6 tr, 2-ch picot, 5 more tr in same sp (shell), skip 1 st,1 sl st in front of shell base* and repeat around. Fasten off at last sl st.

PURSE

Same first six rounds as for the hat top, make two circles. Hold the two circles together, and, using the inner loops, crochet petals as in the hat brim around edge, one round, but crochet two petals on one side only for the opening of the purse. Use dc instead of tr for petals, skipping only 3 st.

Stem Handle

NOTE: The stem handle can be made in any length, if you prefer a longer handle.

ROUND 1: With green, ch 50, turn, in second ch from hk, sc, hdc, 3 dc, hdc, sc, sl st 33, sc, hdc, 3 dc, hdc, 2 sc in last ch, 2-ch picot, 2 more sc in last ch.

ROUND 2: Repeat on the other side of leaf: Hdc, 3 dc, hdc, sc, sl st down to other leaf, sc, hdc, 3 dc, hdc, sc, sl st to end of leaf and fasten off.

Cut 2 feet (61 cm) of green yarn and thread the tapestry needle. Sew the ends of the handle to the purse above the leaves. Press the hat and purse to even out.

These projects were made using 2 skeins (120 yds/109 m) each of Lily's Sugar 'n Cream 4-ply 2.5 ounce (70 g) 100 percent cotton yarn in Yellow #010, White #001, and Sage Green #084.

Sweet Violet and Butterfly

In the garden or on the playground, your delicate flower will get great sun protection and lots of compliments while wearing this hat.

SKILL LEVEL
Intermediate

Size

21 inches (53.3 cm)

Stitches Used

single crochet (sc)
double crochet (dc)
half-double crochet (hdc)
picot stitch

Gauge

3 st = 1 inch (2.3 cm) with G hk

You Will Need

1 skein (120 yds/109 m) worsted weight cotton yarn in light green

1 skein (120 yds/109 m) worsted weight cotton yarn in grape

Scraps of worsted-weight cotton yarn in white and pink for butterfly wings

Size E crochet hook

Size G crochet hook

Stitch marker

Safety pin

HAT

Stem and Sepals

ROUND 1: With green and G hk, ch 4, join to first ch to form circle, ch 1, 5 sc in circle, and place st marker (move st marker to first st of each row from now on).

ROUNDS 2 TO 5: 5 sc in each round, spiraling.

ROUNDS 6 AND 7: 2 sc in ea st around.

ROUND 8: Sc around.

ROUND 9: *Sc, inc, 1 ch, inc, sc* 5 times around.

ROUND 10: *2 sc, hdc, 3 dc in ch-1 sp, hdc, 2 sc* 5 times around.

ROUND 11: *In top loop only, 4 sc, hdc inc, ch-2 picot, hdc inc; 4 sc* 5 times, except on the very last sc, instead make a sl st and fasten off.

Petals

ROUND 12: Using the size G hk for the petals, tie on grape yarn to the next exposed loop on the bottom of the green and ch 1. (Be sure the stem side of green is pointing toward you. Continue to spiral.) 3 sc, *in lower loop of picot, that is, ch sp at end of sepal tip (at hdc cluster) 3 sc, 8 sc*, continue around, but in last set end with 5 sc.

ROUND 13: Starting in ch 1 sp, 5 sc, *3 sc in tip st, 10 sc* 5 times, end with 5 sc.

ROUND 14: *12 sc, 3 sc in tip* around.

ROUND 15: *14 sc, 3 sc in tip* around.

ROUND 16: *16 sc, 3 sc in tip* around.

ROUND 17: *18 sc, 3 sc in tip* around, except after the last 3 sc, 8 sc.

ROUNDS 18 TO 26: *Sk 2 st, 9 sc, 3 sc in tip, 9 sc*.

ROUND 27: Same as round above, except in last 9 sc, only make 8 sc.

ROUND 28: *Sk 2 st, 18 sc* around.

ROUND 29: *Sk 2 st, in lower loop only, sl st 8, 1-ch picot in tip, 8 sl st* around.

Fasten off.

OPTIONAL BUTTERFLY

Body and Antennae

With pink and the G hk, leaving a 2-inch (5.2 cm) tail, ch 9, starting in second ch from hk, 8 sl st back down chain. Fasten off and cut off yarn, leaving a 2-inch (5.2 cm) tail. Pull both tails so they are tight and trim to 1 to 1 ½ inches (2.5 to 3.8 cm). These are the butterfly antennae.

Wings

With white and E hk, sl st into third from last st on the end opposite the antennae.

ROUND 1: Ch 1, sk 1 st, 7 dc inc, sk 1 st, sc, ch 1, turn.

ROUND 2: Sk 1 st, 5 dc inc, sk 1 st, sl st, and fasten off. Make the second wing on the corresponding loops on the next row of loops on the butterfly body. Hide ends and steam iron the wings and antennae so that they flap up. Attach to the hat with a safety pin or a few stitches.

This project was made using 1 skein (120 yds/109 m) each of Sugar 'n Cream 4-ply 2.5 ounce (70 g) 100 percent cotton yarn in Lime #70 and Grape #071.

Squirrel's Best Friend Hat

When the first crisp days of fall arrive, it's time to make a cozy hat for your toddler. This clever acorn design uses the pineapple stitch for the rim—it takes some practice to learn but is well worth the effort.

SKILL LEVEL
Intermediate to Advanced

You Will Need

1 skein (120 yds/109 m) worsted weight cotton yarn in each of the following colors: light brown, dark brown, and sage green

Size F crochet hook

Stitch markers

Tapestry needle

Pattern Notes

A smaller hat may be made by following the note following Round 14.

Size

20 inches (50.8 cm)

Stitches Used

single crochet (sc)
increases (inc)
half double crochet (hdc)
pineapple stitch
triple crochet (tr)
picot stitch
spiraling with stitch markers

Gauge

3 st = 1 inch (2.5 cm)
4 rounds = 1 inch (2.5 cm)

HAT

(starting at top)

ROUND **1:** With light brown, ch 3, sl st in second ch, in first ch make 4 sc, pass behind sl st and make a sc in first sc. Place st marker in this st, and replace it at the beg of each round.

ROUND **2:** Sc around (4 sc).

ROUND **3:** Inc, 2 sc, inc (6 sc).

ROUND **4:** 6 sc around (6 sc).

ROUND **5:** Inc in every st (12 sc).

ROUND **6:** Sc around (12 sc).

ROUND **7:** *Inc, sc* 6 times (18 sc).

ROUND **8:** Sc around.

ROUND **9:** *Inc, sc* around (27 sc).

ROUND **10:** Sc around.

ROUND **11:** *Inc, sc * around, ending with an inc (41 sc).

ROUND **12:** Sc around.

This project was made using 1 skein (120 yds/109 m) each of Lily's Sugar 'n Cream 4-ply 2.5 ounce (70 g) 100 percent cotton yarn in Jute #082, Warm Brown #1130, and Sage Green #084.

ROUND 13: *Inc, 2 sc* around, ending with sc (55 sc).

ROUND 14: Sc around.

NOTE: For a small hat (about 17 to 18 inches [43 to 48 cm]), do not inc in the next round, but start spiraling down to round 25, then join on warm brown yarn and proceed with pineapple stitch.

ROUND 15: *Inc, 3 sc* around, ending with 2 sc (69 sc).

ROUNDS 16 TO 26: Sc around, spiraling down; finish off last 2 st of Round 26 with 2 sl st, fasten off.

ROUNDS 27 TO 29: Join dark brown yarn, ch 4, sk 1 st, begin *pineapple stitch* (see page 16) around, beg round with ch 4.

ROUND 30: Sl st around bottom edge of hat, fasten off.

Leaf (make two)

ROUND 1: With sage green, ch 10, sl st in second ch from hk, sc, sk 1 st, 4 hdc in next ch sp, sk 1 st, sc, sk 1 st, 4 hdc in next ch sp, 1 sl st, turn to go around other side of ch, 4 hdc in sp where other 4 hdc are, sc in other sc sp, 4 hdc in hdc sp, sk st, 2 sl st to end point. Ch 1.

ROUND 2: Working in top loop only, 5 sc, 2-ch picot, sc in same sp, dec, 3 sc, 2-ch picot, sc in same sp, 3 sc, 2-ch picot, sc in same sp, 3 sc, 2-ch picot, sc in same sp, dec, 2 sc, 2-ch picot, sc in same sp, 4 sc, 1 sl st, ch 4 at end for stem, 3 sl st down stem, sl st into base of stem, fasten off.

Sew the leaves on the hat top with the tapestry needle and about 1 foot (30.5) of sage yarn.

Fresh Picks

Tasteful treats for babies
and toddlers, the projects
in this section of the book
are charming and easy
to wear. Whether you're
a beginner or an
experienced crocheter,
you'll find something
to suit your skills
and your baby's style.

Juicy Strawberry Hat

A perfect topper for a summer afternoon, this hat can be pulled down to provide extra sun protection. The seeds may be a little tricky to make because they require carrying two yarns together, so take your time and be patient.

SKILL LEVEL
Advanced

Size

20 to 22 inches (51 to 59 cm)

Stitches Used

single crochet (sc)
half-double crochet (hdc)
double crochet (dc)
triple crochet (tc)
increases (inc)
reverse single crochet (rc)

Gauge

3 stitches = 1 inch (2.5 cm)

You Will Need

1 skein (120 yds/109 m) worsted weight cotton yarn in each of the following colors: red, green, and wine

Size F crochet hook

Stem and Sepals

ROUND 1: With green, ch 8, and starting in second ch from hk, sl st 6. In last ch, 8 sc, join to beg, ch 1.

ROUND 2: *2 sc in ea st* around, join, ch 1.

ROUND 3: Sc around, join, ch 1.

ROUND 4: *Inc, sc* around, join, ch 1.

ROUND 5: Sc around, join.

ROUND 6: Make 6 sepals: *Ch 11, and starting in 2nd ch from hk, 1 sl st, sc, 2 hdc, 3 dc, 2 tr. Sk 3 st and sl st to 4th st on top loop only.* Go around circle and make 6 sepals. 2 sl st, and fasten off green to top loop.

Body of Hat

Join red yarn to bottom loop of last round of green and ch 1. Be sure top of hat is facing you.

ROUND 1: *Inc, sc* around, join, ch 1.

ROUND 2: Sc around, ch 1.

ROUND 3: *Inc, 2 sc* around, ch 1.

ROUND 4: Sc around, ch 1.

ROUND 5: *Inc, 3 sc* around, ch 1.

ROUND 6: Sc around, ch 1.

ROUNDS 7 TO 22: Continuing with red and carrying wine yarn inside st, make a wine colored st every 7 st: 6 red st, 1 wine st for seeds around, staggering the wine stitches and making an unseeded round every other round. You may spiral your rounds. There are no more increases.

LAST ROUND: Rc around in red.

NOTE: You may continue the pattern of increases to make a larger hat for an adult.

This project was made using 1 skein (120 yds/109 m) each of Lily's Sugar 'n Cream 4-ply 2.5 ounce (70 g) 100 percent cotton yarn in Red #095, Wine #015, and Emerald #062.

Pear-fectly Lovely Hat

A sweet topper for a girl or a boy, this luscious pear hat has a rolled brim that can be adjusted to accommodate a growing head.

Size

21 to 23 inches (53.3 to 58.4 cm)
(brim is rolled)

Stitches Used

single crochet (sc)
half-double crochet (hdc)
double crochet (dc)
reverse single crochet (rc)
increases (inc)
spiraling

Gauge

3 st = 1 inch (2.5 cm)
3 rounds = 1 inch (2.5 cm)

You Will Need

1 skein (120 yds/109 m) worsted weight cotton yarn in golden yellow

1 skein (120 yds/109 m) worsted weight cotton yarn in medium green

Size G crochet hook

Stitch markers

Stem and Leaf

With green, ch 9, sl st 8 back down, continue for leaf, ch 10, turn, sl st, sc, hdc, 2 dc hdc, sc, 2 sl to end of leaf, turn work and, working in top loop only, sl st, sc, hdc, 2 dc, hdc, sc, 2 sl st to end, fasten off.

Hat (starting at top)

ROUND 1: In sp between stem and leaf: Join yellow, ch 1, on both sides of this sp, squeeze in 12 sc, join, ch 1. Place st marker so you can spiral down the hat.

ROUND 2: 2 sc in each st except last st, sc (beg ch counts as 1 st).

ROUNDS 3 TO 7: Sc around.

ROUND 8: *Inc, 11 sc* twice.

ROUND 9: Sc around.

ROUND 10: *6 sc, inc* 4 times.

ROUND 11: Sc around.

ROUND 12: *Inc, 4 sc* 6 times.

ROUND 13: Sc around.

ROUND 14: *Inc, 4 sc* 7 times.

ROUND 15: Sc around.

ROUND 16: *Inc, 3 sc*, 10 times, 2 sc.

ROUND 17: Sc around.

ROUND 18: *Inc, 3 sc* 13 times.

ROUNDS 19 TO 39: Sc around.

ROUND 40: Rc edging around.

Fasten off.

This project was made using 1 skein (120 yds/109 m) each of Lily's Sugar 'n Cream 4-ply 2.5 ounce (70 g) 100 percent cotton yarn in Soft Gold #0101 and Dark Pine #071.

Tiny Eggplant Hat and Mitts

Bundle your baby eggplant in a matching hat and mitts for her very first excursions into the world. The hat and mitts can be enlarged by using a larger hook.

SKILL LEVEL
Intermediate

Size

HAT

15 inches (38 cm)

MITTS

Newborn to 3-month size (see page 19)

Stitches Used

single crochet (sc)
half-double crochet (hdc)
double crochet (dc)
triple crochet (tr)
reverse single crochet (rc)
increases (inc)
picot

Gauge

3 st = 1 inch (2.5 cm)

You Will Need

1 skein (120 yds/109 m) worsted weight cotton yarn in light purple

1 skein (120 yds/109 m) worsted weight cotton yarn in sage green

Size F crochet hook

Stitch markers

Pattern Notes

Both the hat and the mitts can be made larger by using a size G crochet hk.

HAT

Stem

ROUND 1: With green, ch 8, turn and starting in second ch from hk, 6 sl st.

ROUND 2: In last st, 6 sc, join to first sc with sl st.

ROUND 3: Ch 2, 2 sc in ea st around, sl st to join.

ROUND 4: Ch 2, sc around, sl st to join.

ROUND 5: Ch 2, *3 sc, 2 sc in next st, repeat from* to end of round (2 sc in every fourth st), join.

ROUND 6: Ch 2, sc in each st to end of round, join.

ROUND 7: Ch 2, 2 sc in every third st, join and do not break off yarn.

Sepal (make four)

Continuing with green, ch 8, turn, work sc in 2nd ch from hk, sc, hdc, dc, tr.

At base of stem, count fourth st from ch and join on top yarn of st only.

Repeat to make three more sepal petals around base of stem, join with sl st, fasten off.

Body of Hat

Join purple yarn at the base of the stem.

ROUND 1: Ch 2, 2 sc in ea st around the base of the stem; under the sepal petals, join.

ROUNDS 2 AND 3: Ch 2, sc around, join.

ROUND 4: Ch 2, *sc in next 3 st, 2 sc in next st, repeat from *, join.

ROUND 5: Ch 2, sc around, join.

ROUND 6: Ch 2, *sc in next 4 st, 2 sc in next st, repeat from *, join.

ROUND 7: Ch 2, sc around, join.

ROUND 8: Ch 2, *sc in next 5 st, 2 sc in next st, repeat from *, join.

NOTE: Continue the pattern of inc here to make a larger hat.

ROUNDS 9 TO 21: Ch 2, sc in each st around.

ROUND 22: Rc in each sc, join, fasten off.

MITT

(make two)

ROUND 1: With purple, ch 5, join into a circle, ch 2, 9 sc into circle, place st marker, ch 1.

ROUND 2: 2 sc in each of next 10 st.

ROUND 3: Spiral down 13 rounds (or more).

Join on green yarn.

ROUND 1: With green, sc around.

ROUND 2: *2 ch, 1 sc* around.

ROUND 3: Sc around. To make larger mitts, 9 sc in ea st.

ROUND 4: *3 sc in one st, 1-ch picot, 3 more sc in same st, sc in next st*, repeat 4 times. To make larger mitts, *inc, 1 sc* all around.

NOTE: For larger mitts, spiral down to the appropriate length.

String Ties with Leaves

With green, ch 6, *1 sl st in first ch from hk, sc, hdc, dc, hdc, sc, 1 sl st*, ch 65; repeat between *.

Finishing

Thread ties through the holes in the mitt cuffs.

This project was made using 1 skein (120 yds/109 m) each of Lily's Sugar 'n Cream 4-ply 2.5 ounce (70 g) 100 percent cotton yarn in Sage Green #082 and Grape #071.

Lovable Zoo

Fluffy, furry, and
downright delightful,
the projects in this section
are sure to be enjoyed by
kids and parents alike.
Toddlers will love to play
make believe disguised as
their favorite animals, and
parents will love to take
their little creatures out in
these adorable ensembles.

Cuddly Calf Hat, Bell, and Hooves

Your barnyard baby will look delightful in this charming ensemble. Make two sets of hooves for hands and feet, or just one if your little creature is likely to remove them!

SKILL LEVEL
Beginner to Intermediate

Sizes

HAT

20 to 21 inches (50.8 to 53.3 cm)

HOOVES

9- to 12- month size (see page 19)

Stitches Used

single crochet (sc)
increases (inc)
decreases (dec)
spiraling

Gauge

3 stitches = 1 inch (2.5 cm)
3 st rounds = 1 inch (2.5 cm)

You Will Need

1 skein (120 yards/109 m) worsted weight cotton yarn in each of the following colors: white, black, soft gold

Size G crochet hook

2 black or white buttons, each about ¾ inch (1.9 cm) in diameter

Tapestry needle

Stitch markers

HAT (starting at top)

ROW 1: With white, ch 13, starting in second ch from hk, sc 12, ch 1 and turn.

ROWS 2 TO 27: Sc 12, ch 1, turn at the end of each row.

ROW 28: Dec, sc across, ch 1, turn.

ROW 29: Sc across, ch 1, turn.

ROW 30: Sc across except in last st, dec, ch 1, turn.

ROW 31: Sc across.

ROWS 32 TO 35: Repeat rows 28 to 31.

ROWS 36 TO 37: Repeat rows 28 and 29, do not ch 1, fasten off.

Hat Side (make two)

Ch 1 and turn at the end of each row, unless otherwise stated.

ROW 1: With black, ch 2, 6 sc in first ch.

ROW 2: 2 sc in ea st across (12 sc).

ROW 3: Sc across.

ROW 4: *Inc, sc* across.

ROW 5: Sc across, but only make 17 stitches. Do not make the last st. Mark the end of this row, as you will be leaving off 1 st at this end of the non-increase rows.

ROW 6: *2 sc, inc* 5 times, then 2 sc.

ROW 7: 21 sc across row (do not make last st).

ROW 8: *3 sc, inc* 5 times, then 1 sc.

ROW 9: 25 sc across row (no last st).

ROW 10: *4 sc, inc* 5 times, sc.

ROW 11: 28 sc across.

ROW 12: *5 sc, inc* 4 times, then 4 sc.

ROW 13: 31 sc across.

ROW 14: *6 sc, inc* 4 times, 2 sc, 1 sl st.

ROW 15: Sk 1 st, 33 sc across.

ROW 16: 21 sc, 1 sl st, fasten off.

Putting the Hat Together

The long non-curved side is the front of the hat. Clip the sides to the white middle with the tapering end of the white top in the back. Hold it in place with little hair clips, if you like. Thread about 2 feet (61 cm) of white yarn on the tapestry needle. When sewing the sides to the top, remember that one sc matches up with the side of one row.

When the top has been sewn to the sides, make a 2-row sc border: With white, beg at back of hat on white part, sc to front corner, 3 sc in each front corner. Go around hat twice for border.

Horn (make two)

ROUND 1: With soft gold (leaving a 6-inch [15.2 cm]) tail of yarn to sew horn onto hat), ch 10 and join to form circle, ch 1. 10 sc around circle.

ROUND 2: Starting in first sc, 10 sc around.

ROUND 3: *3 sc, dec* 2 times.

ROUND 4: 7 sc.

ROUND 5: *2 sc, dec* 3 times, sc. Snip off yarn leaving a 5- or 6-inch (12.7 to 15.2-cm) tail. Fasten off.

Sew the top of the horn with one stitch and fasten off. Sew onto the top of the hat: Place the horns on lines between the black and white, 4 rounds back from front of the hat, starting sts at the back of the horn.

Ear (make two)

ROW 1: With white, leaving a 6-inch (15.2 cm) tail, ch 8, starting in second ch from hk, 7 sc, ch 1, turn.

ROWS 2 TO 9: 7 sc in each row. Ch 1, turn at the end of each row except Row 9, do not ch, just turn work.

ROW 10: Sk 1 st, 1 sl st, 3 sc, 2 sl st, turn.

ROW 11: Ch 1, sk 1 st, 1 sl st, 2 sc, 2 sl st.

ROW 12: Ch 1, sk 1 st, 1 sl st, sc, 2 sl st.

ROW 13: Ch 1, sk 1 st, 1 sl st, sc, 1-ch picot, 1 sl st, fasten off.

Thread the tapestry needle and sew the two long sides of the ear tog at the base for 4 rows. Fasten off. Edge the ear opening with 1 round of black sc, making an sc at the end of each row as you go around, 3 sc at ear tip picot. Fasten off. Sew on the ears firmly just below the horns.

Cowbell

ROUND 1: With soft gold, ch 9, join to form loop, ch 4, join to form smaller loop (you now have a lopsided figure 8). Ch 1, make 8 sc in smaller loop. Place marker and begin to spiral rounds.

ROUND 2: *Inc, 3 sc* 2 times around.

ROUND 3: 12 sc around.

ROUND 4: *Inc, 4 sc* 2 times around.

ROUND 5: 14 sc around.

ROUND 6: *Inc, 5 sc* 2 times around, sc, 2 sl st, fasten off.

Chin Strap and Buttons

For the chin strap, ch 39, in third ch from hk, dc across row, fasten off, slip on the cowbell. Sew on the buttons at the bottom front corners of hat. Button on the strap.

NOTE: The calf chin strap is adjustable—button it onto any hole in the strap.

HOOF

(make two, or four if you want mitts and hooves)

ROUND 1: With black, ch 4, join to first ch to form circle, sc 12 in circle, piece is made in a spiral.

ROUND 2: (Place a st marker in first st of each round.) 2 sc in ea around (24 st).

ROUNDS 3 AND 4: Sc around.

ROUND 5: Working in top loop for this round only: Sc around.

ROUNDS 6 TO 10: Sc around.

ROUNDS 11 TO 14: With white, sc around.

ROUND 15: Make holes for ties: Ch 2, *skip 1 st, dc, ch 1* 10 times, around, joining to ch 2 as last st.

ROUNDS 16 TO 19: Sc around.

ROUND 20: Make shells around: *Sk 2 st, 6 dc in one sp, sk 2 st, sc* 4 times, but instead, on last sc, sl st into last sc of previous round. Fasten off.

Tie
(make one for each mitt and hoof)

With white, ch 60, sl st back along top loop of ch, fasten off.

NOTE: Hoof mitts may be made larger by making an increase round for Row 5: *inc, 2 sc* to end of row. Row 6: 1 sc in each st. Continue with the same instructions after Row 6.

This project was made using 1 skein (120 yards [109 ml) each of Lily's Sugar 'n Cream 4-ply 2.5 ounce (70 g) 100 percent cotton yarn in White #001, Black #002, and Soft Gold #0101.

Busy Bumble Bee Hat

SKILL LEVEL

Intermediate

A cute hat like this will create quite a buzz wherever your little bee is seen. The design keeps ears covered and ensures that the hat will stay put on a busy bee's head, even when he or she wants it off.

Size

20 inches (51 cm)

Stitches Used

single crochet (sc)

Gauge

(average between the yellow worsted and the chunky chenille)

WORSTED
4 stitches =
1 inch (2.5 cm)
3 rounds =
1 inch (2.5 cm)

CHENILLE
2 stitches = 1 inch (2.5 cm)
3 rounds = 1 ¾ inches (4 cm)

You Will Need

1 skein (120 yds/109 m) worsted weight acrylic yarn in yellow

1 skein (120 yds/109 m) worsted weight acrylic yarn in black

1 skein (100 yds/91 m) chenille yarn in black

Size G crochet hook (for hat)

Size E crochet hook (for antennae)

Tapestry needle

Purchased black pompoms (optional)

Washable fabric glue

Pattern Notes

This hat is worked in top loops only in black and both loops in yellow. The color pattern is two rounds of black, three rounds of yellow. When you work in black chenille, it can be hard to see where to place your hk for the next stitch—just go by feel and count your stitches.

HAT

(starting at top)

ROUND **1:** With black chenille and the size G hk, ch 6, join to form circle, ch 1, 12 sc in circle, ch 1.

ROUND **2:** 2 sc in each st (24 st around), join to first ch with yellow yarn. You don't have to cut yarn at color changes: you may leave it to use for the next stripe.

ROUND **3:** *2 sc in each st* 24 times, join to first ch and ch 1 (48 st).

ROUND **4**: Sc around, join to first ch, ch 1.

ROUND **5:** Sc around, join to first ch with black, ch 1.

ROUND **6:** Sc (48 st) in black around, ch 1.

ROUND **7:** Sc around, join with yellow, ch 1.

ROUND **8:** Sc in yellow around, ch 1.

ROUND **9:** Sc in yellow around, ch 1.

ROUND **10:** Sc in yellow around, join with black at end of round, ch 1.

Continue to alternate two rounds black, three rounds yellow, 48 st in each round until you have a total of four black stripes and four yellow stripes. Fasten off after the last yellow stripe is finished.

Antenna (make two)

Use black acrylic and the size E hk. Crochet the stitches very loosely and you may use the front loop of the stitches only if it's easier. Leaving a 12-inch (30.5 cm) tail of yarn, ch 7, join to first ch to form circle, ch 1, in top loops of ch, 6 sc and beg to spiral. Stitches will be counted, rather than rounds. Spiral up 20 more st, dec. Then make 13 more st and one more dec. Make six more st, dec, and fasten off. Thread the tail of yarn onto the tapestry needle and sew the antennae onto the first black stripe of the hat.

Pompom (make two)

Use the black acrylic yarn and see instructions for making a pompom on page 22 or use purchased pompoms. Glue the pompoms onto the ends of the antennae.

This project was made using 1 skein (120 yds/109 m) of Lion Brand's 8 ounce (220 g) Thick-and-Quick Chenille in Black #153, 1 skein (120 yds/109 m) of Coats and Clark's Red Heart 4-ply 3 ounce (85 g) acrylic yarn in Bright Yellow # 0324, and 1 skein (120 yds/109 m) of Mainstays' 4-ply 8 ounce (220 gram) acrylic yarn in True Black #108.

Friendly Lion Hat and Mitts

With a fluffy mohair mane and soft merino wool mitts, this lion is anything but fierce. Use this set as part of a Halloween costume or just to keep your little wild thing warm.

SKILL LEVEL
Advanced

Size

HAT
22 to 23 inches (56 to 58.5 cm)

MITTS
9- to 12-month size (see page 19)

Stitches Used

single crochet (sc)
loop stitch (loop st)
half-double crochet (hdc)
double-crochet (dc)
picot stitch
spiraling
running stitch

Gauge

FOR HAT AND MITTS
4 ½ st = 1 inch (2.5 cm)

FOR MANE
3 ½ st = 1 inch (2.5 cm)

You Will Need

1 skein (85 yds/78 m) worsted weight merino wool in gold

1 skein (89 yds/81 m) fingering weight mohair in tan

Scrap yarn in black for embroidery

Size I crochet hook

Stitch markers

¾-inch (1.9 cm) button for strap

Tapestry needle

HAT

(starting at back)

ROW 1: With gold, ch 15. Starting in third ch from hk, dc 11, in last st of ch, make 6 dc. Dc 12 down other side of ch, ch 2, turn.

ROW 2: Dc down row to cluster of 6 dc. 2 dc in each st of cluster. Dc down other side to end, ch 2, turn.

ROW 3: Dc around, ch 2, turn.

ROW 4: 12 dc to cluster, *inc, dc* 6 times, continue to dc (11 dc) down other side, ch 2, turn.

ROW 5: Dc around, ch 2, turn.

ROWS 6 TO 10: Dc 12, *inc, 2 dc* 6 times, dc to end of row, ch 1, turn.

ROW 11: Sc around, ch 1 only, turn.

ROWS 7 TO 14: Dc around, ch 2, turn.

Turn the hat so ch 1 is on your right. Make 1 sl st at the end of each row of dc, along the bottom edge, skipping center chain. Fasten off.

Mane

Attach tan where you fastened off, ch 1. Loop st along the front of the hat. Do 7 rows of loop st, ending with the loops. Do not fasten off. Ch 1, turn work.

Chin Strap

7 loop st across the bottom of one side of the mane. Ch 1, turn. Next row, dec at first and last st. Continue loop st back and forth on the neck strap for 15 rows. Fasten off. Tie the button on the end of the strap. It can be buttoned in any available loop inside the mane.

Ear (make two)

ROW 1: With gold, ch 2 and in second ch from hk, 8 hdc, ch 2, turn.

ROW 2: 2 hdc across, ch 1.

ROW 3 (BOTTOM OF EAR ONLY): Sc at the ends of all the rows, fasten off leaving a 1-foot (30.5 cm) tail of yarn.

Sew on the ears with the tapestry needle. Find the center of the hat on the last row of dc, right where the loops start. Count over 4 st on each side of center st, sew on ears 9 dc apart.

MITT

(make two)

ROUND 1: With gold, ch 5, join to first ch to make circle, ch 1, 12 sc in circle, join, ch 1.

ROUND 2: 2 sc in each st around, join, ch 1.

ROUND 3: Sc around, join, ch 1.

ROUND 4: *Inc, 3 sc* repeat around, place a st marker here, do not join, but start to spiral rounds.

ROUNDS 5 TO 19: Place st marker here at beg of round, sc around.

ROUND 20: *Ch 2, sk 1 st, sc*, around for drawstring loops.

ROUND 21: *In each ch-2 sp, 3 sc* around.

ROUND 22: *Sc, sk 2 st, 5 dc in one st, sk 2 st (shell st)* repeat around. Fasten off.

Lion Head and Tail Ties for Mitts

With gold, ch 70, in second to last st, 4 sc, 2-ch picot, 2 sc, 2-ch picot, 4 sc, sl st into first sc to make lion head. Sl st down entire length of chain, fasten off.

Join tan to the other end of the tie, ch 1, 4 sc, ch 1, turn, 2 sc in 2 center st, ch 1, turn, sc, fasten off.

On the head end, join tan to next outer loop of circle near ch. 2 sc in each outer loop of head, going behind ears and around, stop short of neck and fasten off.

With black scrap yarn, sew three long lines in running stitch (see page 20) around the ends of the paws.

This project was made using 1 skein (85 yds/78 m) of Mission Falls 1.75 ounce (50 g) 100 percent merino superwash-wool yarn in Curry #13 and 1 skein (89 yds/81 m) of Ironstone English Mohair 2 ounce (57 g) mohair yarn in Maize #832.

Fifi the Poodle Hat and Mitts

Très adorable! This one is a real show-stopper. To help the poodle's poof retain its perfectly round shape, you may want to stuff it with a little fiberfill or other lightweight material.

SKILL LEVEL
Advanced

Size

HAT
19 inches (48.3 cm)

MITTS
Newborn to 3-month size
(see page 19)

Stitches Used

single crochet (sc)
loop stitch (loop st) with two yarns
half-double crochet (hdc)
reverse single crochet (rc)
slip stitch (sl st)
increases (inc)
decreases (dec)

Gauge

WITH BOTH YARNS TOG. AND J HK
3 st = 1 inch (2.5 cm)
2 ½ rows – 1 inch (2.5 cm)

WITH ACRYLIC WORSTED AND G HK
3 ½ st = 1 inch (2.5 cm)
3 rows = 1 inch (2.5 cm)

You Will Need

1 skein (120 yds/109 m) worsted weight acrylic yarn in pale pink

1 skein (77 yards/70 m) eyelash yarn in pink

Size J crochet hook

Size G crochet hook

Tapestry needle

Pattern Notes

Crocheting with two yarns tog, may seem difficult, but keeping your stitches loose will make it easier. You may spiral these rounds. For instructions on the loop st, see page 16.

HAT

Top and Sides of Hat

ROUND 1: Using the J hk and holding both yarns tog, ch 4, join to form circle, ch 1, 10 loop st in circle, join, ch 1.

ROUND 2: 2 loop st in each st around, join, ch 1.

ROUNDS 3 AND 4: Loop st in each st around, join, ch 1.

ROUND 5 (ALL IN LOOP ST): Inc, 6 st, inc, 6 st, inc, 6 st, join, ch 1.

ROUNDS 6 TO 9: Loop st in every st around, join and ch 1 at the end of each round.

ROUND 10: Cut off eyelash yarn and switch to size G hk and all sc. *Inc, 2 sc* around. Ch 1 and turn hat so the opening is pointing away from you.

ROW 11: *2 sc in ea st* 15 times, leaving face opening in the front. Ch 1, turn.

ROW 12: *Inc, 4 sc* 6 times across, ch 1, turn.

ROWS 13 TO 27: Sc across, ch 1, turn.

ROW 28: 10 sc, dec, 5 sc, dec, 5 sc, dec, 10 sc, ch 1, turn.

ROW 29: 15 sc, dec, 16 sc, ch 1, turn.

ROWS 30 AND 31: Sc across, ch 1, turn.

ROW 32: Sc across.

ROW 33 (MAKES TIES AND EDGING): Ch 45, sl st back along ch, sc at the end of each round along the front side of the hat (17 sc), hdc, 2 dc in the corner where the side meets the fluffy top. Going across the forehead, hdc, 9 sc, hdc, 2 dc in the corner where the top meets the side, hdc, 17 sc down the side. Ch 45, sl st along ch, sl st along the bottom of the back of the hat, fasten off at the tie.

Ear (make two)

ROW 1: Starting at top and using the size G hk, hold both yarns tog, ch 6, starting in second ch from the hk, 5 sc, ch 1, turn.

ROW 2: 5 loop st across, ch 1, turn.

ROWS 3 TO 6: Repeat rows 1and 2, turn.

ROW 7: Inc, 4 sc, ch 1, turn.

ROW 8: 6 loop st, ch 1, turn.

ROW 9: 5 sc, inc, ch 1, turn.

ROW 10: 7 loop st, ch 1, turn.

ROW 11: Inc, 6 sc, ch 1, turn.

ROW 12: 8 loop st, ch 1, turn.

ROW 13: 7 sc, inc, ch 1, turn.

ROW 14: 9 loop st, ch 1, turn.

ROW 15: 9 sc, ch 1.

ROW 16: 9 loop st, ch 1.

ROW 17: Dec, 5 sc, dec, ch 1.

ROW 18: 7 loop st, ch 1.

ROW 19: Dec, 3 sc, dec. Fasten off.

This is the bottom of the ear.

Finishing

Cut 2 feet (61 cm) of pink acrylic and thread onto the tapestry needle. Sew the ears on the hat at each side, on the second pink acrylic round down, 2 sts in.

Pompom for Ends of Ties (make two)

Cut 2-foot (61 cm) long strands of plain pink yarn, set aside for tying pompoms. Holding both kinds of yarns tog, wind around two fingers seven times loosely and cut. Place the bundle on one of the strands and tie tightly in a square knot. Clip the loops open and fluff. Trim to a pompom shape. Using strands, tie a pompom to each end of the tie.

MITT

(make two)

ROUND **1:** Using both yarns tog and the size J hk, ch 5, join to first ch to form loop, ch 1, 12 sc into loop, join, ch 1.

ROUND **2:** *Inc, 3 sc* 3 times, join, ch 1.

ROUNDS **3** TO **7:** 15 sc, join, ch 1.

ROUND **8:** Snip off eyelash yarn. With plain pink, 15 sc, join to ch 1, ch 3.

ROUND **9:** *Sk st, dc, ch 1* 7 times, join to ch 3, ch 1.

ROUND **10:** 15 sc around in top loop only, join, ch 1.

ROUND **11:** 15 rc, fasten off.

Tie for Mitts (make two)

Ch 50, fasten off. Weave the ties through dc/ch holes in the wrists of the mitts.

This project was made using 1 skein (77 yds/70 m) of Bernat's 1.75 ounce (50 g) 100 percent nylon eyelash yarn in Kiss and 1 skein (120 yds/109 m) of Mainstays', 4-ply 8 ounce (227 g) 100 percent acrylic yarn in Pale Pink.

Frisky Whiskers Cat Hat

The oh-so-soft alpaca yarn used for this hat makes it extra warm and snuggly. The playful design elements, such as the cat heads on the ties, make it fun to wear.

Size

19 inches (48.3 cm)

Stitches Used

single crochet (sc)
half-double crochet (hdc)
double crochet (dc)
overlay stitch (overlay st)
picot

Gauge

4 st = 1 inch (2.5 cm)

You Will Need

1 skein (105 yds/96 m) sport weight alpaca yarn in light tan

1 skein (105 yds/96 m) sport weight alpaca yarn in black

Size F crochet hook

Tapestry needle

SKILL LEVEL
Intermediate

Pattern Notes

See note on page 18 for information about making shells.

Hat Body (starting at back)

ROW 1: With tan, ch 17, starting in third ch from hk, dc 13, in last st of ch, 6 dc (shell). Dc 13 down other side of ch. Ch 3, turn.

ROW 2: Dc in ea st to cluster of 6 dc (shell), 2 dc in each st of cluster. Dc down other side to end. Ch 3, turn.

ROW 3: Dc across (35 st). Ch 3, turn.

ROW 4: 12 dc to shell, *dc inc, 1 dc* 6 times, continue to dc (12 dc) down other side. Ch 3, turn.

ROW 5: Dc around, ch 3, turn.

ROW 6: Dc 13, *dc inc, 2 dc* 6 times, dc 14 to end of row. Ch 3, turn.

ROWS 7 TO 12: Dc around, ch 3 and turn at the end of each row. Fasten off.

Whiskers and Face

ROW 1: Attach black yarn to the lower right front corner of the hat. Ch 1, 3 sc, make next st with an overlay st down 1 row, sc, overlay st 2 rows, sc, overlay st 3 rows, sc, overlay st 2 rows, sc, overlay st 1 row, 4 sc, overlay st 1 row, sc, overlay st 1 row, 15 sc, overlay st 1 row, sc, overlay st 1 row, 4 sc, overlay st 1 row, sc, 1 overlay st 2 rows, sc, overlay st 3 rows, sc, overlay st 2 rows, sc, overlay st 1 row, 2 sc, ch 1, turn.

ROWS 2 AND 3: Sc across, ch 1, turn.

ROW 4: 24 sc, 2 hdc, 3 dc in one sp, 2 hdc, 24 sc, ch 1, turn.

ROW 5: 25 sc, 2 hdc, 3 dc in one sp, 2 hdc, 24 sc, sc in last st, ch 1, turn.

ROW 6: 1 sl st in each st across, except in the very middle st, 1-ch picot. Do not fasten off at end of row. Turn work so that your hk is on your right and you are prepared to crochet across bottom of hat. Ch 1.

Bottom of Hat

ROW 1: Sc across the bottom edge of the hat at the ends of all the rows, sc for every sc row, and 2 sc for every dc row (approx 52 st). Ch 1, turn.

ROW 2: Make holes along the bottom edge of hat for the drawstring. Ch 5, *sk 2 st, dc, ch 3* across the bottom of the hat. Ch 1, turn.

ROW 3: Sc across. Fasten off.

Ear (make two)

ROW 1: With black, ch 5, in fourth ch from hk, make 6 dc, ch 3, turn.

ROW 2: 3 dc; in center st, 3 dc, 2-ch picot, 3 dc; 4 dc.

Leaving a 9-inch (23 cm) tail, fasten off. Sew the ears onto the hat with the yarn tail and tapestry needle. Using the eyebrow whiskers as guides, sew the ears on the next row, making ears about 8 st apart.

Kitty Head for Tie (make two)

With black, ch 4 and join to first ch to form circle. Ch 2 and in circle, 8 hdc, ch 3, in first ch, sc (to make ear), 3 hdc in circle, ch 3 with 1 sc in first ch to make the other ear, 5 hdc in circle. Join to top of first st. Fasten off. For the whiskers, cut a 4-inch (10 cm) piece of black yarn and tie in a square knot to an st below the center hole where the kitty nose would be. Fan out the ply of the yarn and cut to desired length. Whiskers may be woven under an outer st to hold in place.

Tie

With black, ch 140, turn and sc all along single top loop of ch to other end. Fasten off leaving a 3-inch (7.6 cm) tail. Weave the tie through the loops at the bottom edge of the hat. Sew the kitty heads on the ends.

This project was made using 1 skein (105 yds/96 m) each of Reynolds Andean Alpaca Classic 4-ply 3.5 ounce (100 g) alpaca yarn in Black #106 and Light Tan #21.

Sweet Treats

Sweet as can be,

the projects in this section

are a treat to make and

a delight for kids to wear.

Finish one project,

and you'll be ready

for seconds!

Single Scoop Hat

Give your favorite tot her heart's desire—a big scoop of ice cream with a cherry on top. The recipe for this little treat starts with all-cotton yarn, and it's easy enough for a beginner to make.

SKILL LEVEL
Easy

Size

20 inches (50.8 cm)

Stitches Used

single crochet (sc)
reverse crochet (rc)
embroidery

Gauge

4 sts = 1 inch (2.5 cm)

You Will Need

1 skein (100 yds/91.4 m) worsted weight cotton yarn in white

1 skein (100 yds/91.4 m) worsted weight cotton yarn in soft gold

Red yarn scraps for cherry or purchased red pompom

Size G hook

Stitch marker

Tapestry needle

HAT

(starting at the top)

ROUND 1: With white, ch 5, join to form circle, ch 1, 8 sc in circle. Place st marker to remember beg of rounds. The hat is crocheted in a spiral.

ROUND 2: 2 sc in each st.

ROUNDS 3 AND 4: Sc around.

ROUND 5: *Inc, sc* around, 8 times.

ROUNDS 6 AND 7: Sc around

ROUND 8: *Inc, 2 sc* around row, 8 times.

ROUNDS 9 TO 10: Sc around.

ROUND 11: *Inc, 3 sc* around.

ROUNDS 12 AND 13: Sc around.

ROUND 14: *Inc, 4 sc* around.

ROUNDS 15 AND 16: Sc around

ROUND 17: *Inc, 5 sc* around.

ROUNDS 18 AND 19: Sc around.

ROUND 20: *Inc, 6 sc* around.

ROUNDS 21 AND 22: Sc around, making last two sts in sl st to even off the hat bottom, fasten off.

Beg the cone band at bottom of the hat (you should have 64 sc around). This part is not crocheted in a spiral, but join and ch 1 at the end of each round.

ROUNDS 1: Tie soft gold yarn onto back loop of last white row and sc all around row in back loops only. Join, and ch 1.

ROUND 2: Rc around, on front loop only, join and ch 1.

ROUND 3: On back loop, sc around, join and ch 1.

ROUNDS 4 TO 10: Sc around, join, and ch 1 at the end of each round.

ROUND 11: Rc around, fasten off.

Embroidery of Waffle Cone Criss-Crosses

Cut five 40-inch (1 m) strands of soft gold yarn and thread one onto the tapestry needle. Beginning at the back, make 2 rows of X in running stitch. Using the stitches as your guide, make the Xs 4 rows high and 4 stitches wide. Make one row of plain stitches between the rows.

Make (see page 22) a pompom or sew a purchased pompom to the top of the hat with few back stitches and the tapestry needle (see page 21).

This project was made using 1 skein (100 yds/91.4 m) each of Lily's Sugar 'n Cream 4-ply 2.5 ounce (70 g) 100 percent cotton yarn in White #001 and Soft Gold #0101.

Candy Kiss Hat

This easy-to-make hat is the perfect accessory for a kissable tot. Write or embroider "kiss me" on the top ribbon for an extra-special touch.

SKILL LEVEL

Beginner

Size

15 inches (38 cm)

Stitches Used

single crochet (sc)
increases (inc)

Gauge

5 stitches = 1 inch (2.5 cm)
3 rows = 1¾ inches (4.4 cm)

You Will Need

1 skein (115 yards/105 m) worsted weight silver metallic yarn in silver

Size E crochet hook

Stitch markers

White satin ribbon, 8 x 1-inch (20.3 x 2.5 cm) wide

Needle and white thread

ROUND 1: Ch 5, join to form circle, ch 1, 8 sc in circle, do not join, place marker so you can spiral this project, move marker to next round at the end of each round.

ROUND 2: *Inc, sc* around, 4 times.

ROUNDS 3 AND 4: Sc around.

ROUND 5: *Inc, 5 sc* 2 times.

ROUND 6: Sc around.

ROUND 7: *Inc, 6 sc* 2 times.

ROUND 8: Sc around.

ROUND 9: *Inc, 5 sc* 2 times, 3 sc.

ROUND 10: Sc around.

ROUND 11: *Inc, 6 sc* 2 times, inc, 4 sc.

ROUND 12: Sc around.

ROUND 13: *Inc, 5 sc* 3 times, inc, 3 sc.

ROUND 14: Sc around.

ROUND 15: *Inc, 6 sc* 3 times, inc, 4 sc.

ROUND 16: Sc around.

ROUND 17: *Inc, 3 sc* 7 times, inc, 1 sc.

ROUND 18: Sc around.

ROUND 19: *Inc, 4 sc* 7 times, inc, 2 sc.

ROUND 20: Sc around (46 sts).

ROUND 21: *Inc, 4 sc* 9 times, plus 1 sc.

ROUND 22: Sc around.

ROUND 23: *Inc, 4 sc* 11 times.

ROUND 24: Sc around.

ROUND 25: *Inc, 6 sc* 9 times, inc, 2 sc.

ROUND 26: Sc around.

ROUND 27: *Inc, 5 sc* 12 times, inc, 2 sc.

ROUNDS 28 TO 38: Sc around.

ROUND 39: Sl st in each st, fasten off.

Pull the white ribbon through the hole at the top of the hat and secure it on the inside with a few stitches.

This project was made using 1 skein (115 yds/105 m) of Lion Brand's Glitterspun 1.75 ounce (50 g) acrylic yarn in Silver #150.

Peppermint Candy Hat and Scarf

This matching hat and scarf set is eye candy for your toddler! The cotton yarn makes it flexible and cozy for a little one who usually protests being bundled.

Size

HAT
18 inches (45.7 cm)
(See Round 19 for 21-inch [53.3 cm] size)

Stitches Used

single crochet (sc)
increases (inc)
decreases (dec)

Gauge

3 st = 1 inch (2.5 cm)

You Will Need

1 skein (120 yds/109 m) worsted weight cotton yarn in red

1 skein (120 yds/109 m) worsted weight cotton yarn in white

Size G crochet hook

Pattern Notes

Color changing is easy once you get the hang of it. Use the white like you ordinarily would and hold the red on top of the stitches, crocheting around it. When it comes time to change to red, there is no need to let go of the yarns: simply weave your hook around the white yarn to pick up the red. The directions at first tell you to pull through the new color on the last part of the sc, but omit this reminder after Round 5. From then on, remember to start your color change on the previous st.

HAT

ROUND 1: With white, ch 6, join to first ch to make circle, ch 1, 12 sc in circle, ch 1, place st marker.

ROUND 2: 2 sc in each sc around (24 st), ch 1.

ROUND 3: Pick up the red yarn and carry it inside the white stitches and begin color changes: *2 white sc, white sc with red pulled through final loop, red sc with white pulled through final loop* 6 times around, ch 1 in white.

ROUND 4: *White inc, sc, inc, but in second sc pull through red, sc in red with white pulled through at end* around, 6 times, ch 1 in white.

ROUND 5: *4 white sc, 2 red sc* 6 times, ch 1 in white.

ROUND 6: *Starting in white, inc, 2 sc, inc, in red 2 sc* around, ch 1 in white.

ROUND 7: *5 white sc, 3 red sc* 6 times, ch 1 in white.

ROUND 8: * With white, *inc, 3 sc, inc in red, 3 sc* 6 times, ch 1 in white.

ROUND 9: *6 white sc, 4 red sc* 6 times, ch 1 in white.

ROUND 10: *In white, inc, 4 sc, inc, in red 4 sc* 6 times, ch 1 in white.

ROUND 11: *7 white sc, 5 red sc* 6 times, ch 1 in white.

ROUND 12: *In white, inc, 5 sc, inc, in red 5 sc* 6 times, ch 1 in white.

ROUND 13: *8 white sc, 6 red sc* 6 times, ch 1 in white.

ROUND 14: *In white, inc, 6 sc, inc, in red, 6 sc* 6 times, ch 1 in white.

ROUND 15: *9 white sc, 7 red sc* 6 times, ch 1 in white.

ROUND 16: *In white, inc, 7 sc, inc, in red 7 sc* 6 times, ch 1 in white.

ROUND 17: *10 white sc, 8 red sc* 6 times, ch 1 in white.

ROUND 18: *In white, inc, 8 sc, inc, in red 8 sc* 6 times, ch 1 in white.

ROUND 19: *11 white sc, 9 red sc* 6 times, ch 1 in white.

NOTE: Beg dec here in white to shape the beret for an 18-inch (45.7 cm) (6- to 9-month) size (see page 48). You may also continue the pattern for increasing and make a 21-inch (53.3 cm) hat for a toddler with one more round of inc here.

ROUND 20: *In white, dec, 7 sc, dec, in red 9 sc* 6 times, ch 1 in white.

ROUND 21: *9 white sc, 9 red sc* 6 times, ch 1 in white.

ROUND 22: *In white, dec, 7 sc, in red, dec, 7 sc* 6 times, ch 1 in white.

ROUND 23: *8 white sc, 8 red sc* 6 times, ch 1 in white.

ROUND 24: *In white, dec, 6 sc, in red, dec, 6 sc* 6 times, ch 1 in white.

ROUND 25: *7 white sc, 7 red sc* 6 times, ch 1 in white.

ROUND 26: *In white, dec, 5 sc, in red, dec, 5 sc* 6 times, ch 1 in white.

ROUND 27: *6 white sc, 6 red sc* 6 times, ch 1 in white.

ROUND 28: *In white, dec, 4 sc, in red, dec, 4 sc* 6 times, ch 1 in white.

ROUND 29: *5 white sc, 5 red sc* 6 times, ch 1 in white.

NOTE: Stop dec here for a 21-inch (53.3 cm) hat. Just fasten off.

ROUND 30: *In white, dec, 3 sc, in red dec, 3 sc* 6 times, ch 1 in white.

ROUND 31: *4 white sc, 4 red sc* 6 times, ch 1 in white.

NOTE: Stop here for an 18-inch (45.7 cm) hat. Fasten off.

SCARF

Pattern Notes

The scarf's diagonal stripes are easy to make, and you will quickly recognize the pattern: all single inc at one edge, all single dec at the other edge, nine white rows, six red ones. This makes the scarf curl up into a tube just like a peppermint stick.

ROW 1: In white, ch 3, in second ch from hk, 3 sc, ch 1, turn.

ROW 2: Inc, sc, inc, ch 1, turn.

ROW 3: Inc, 3 sc, inc, ch 1 turn.

ROW 4: Inc, 5 sc, inc, ch 1 turn.

ROW 5: Inc, 7 sc, inc, ch 1, turn.

ROW 6: Inc, 9 sc, inc, ch 1, turn.

ROW 7: Inc, 11 sc, inc, ch 1, turn.

ROW 8: Inc, 13 sc, inc, ch 1, turn.

ROW 9: Inc, 15 sc, inc, ch 1 in red, turn. Continue for 6 rows in red.

ROW 10: Inc, 17 sc, inc, ch 1, turn.

ROW 11: Inc, 17 sc, dec, ch 1, turn.

ROW 12: Dec, 17 sc, inc, ch 1, turn.

ROW 13: Inc, 17 sc, dec, ch 1, turn.

ROW 14: Dec, 17 sc, inc, ch 1, turn.

ROW 15: Inc, 17 sc, dec, ch 1 in white, turn.

ROW 16: Dec, 17 sc, inc, ch 1, turn.

NOTE: By now you can probably see the pattern, so just continue to desired length, or 48 inches (1.2 m) which would be eight red stripes and nine white ones, beginning and ending with white.

LAST (WHITE) STRIPE: Dec on both ends of nine rows to form squared-off end. Fasten off.

This project was made using 1 skein (120 yds/109 ml) each of Lily's Sugar 'n Cream 4-ply 2.5 ounce (70 g) 100 percent cotton yarn in Red #95 and White #001.

ACKNOWLEDGMENTS

I would like to thank: Nana, for teaching me to crochet; Cindy Lou Travers for asking me to make that first tomato hat; and Johnny Preston for his constant support and inspiring paintings. Thanks also to all my friends at Lark Books, especially Joanne O'Sullivan.

Thank you so much also to the baby models and their parents! You really made the book.

Ethan Gage Banks
Seth Lambert Bellamy
Allison Leigh Caskey
Lillian Wynn Chase
Thomas Griffiths Dickson
Coulson Timothy Dunning
Wyatt C. Dunning
Sophia Frank-Garcia
Maeve Frances Goldberg
Zella Sky Jackson
Sarah Grace McCartney
Owen Henry Alexander McMahon
Hannah Elizabeth Mosher
Nicholas Charles Mosrie
Keagan Blue Ocean
Elizabeth Ellyn Patteson
Oona Chaoli Silverstein
Emily Laurel Stokes
Jamonty Ahmad Williams

METRIC CONVERSION

Inches	Mm	Cm
½	13	1.3
⅝	16	1.6
¾	19	1.9
⅞	22	2.2
1	25	2.5
1¼	32	3.2
1½	38	3.8
1¾	44	4.4
2	51	5.1
2½	64	6.4
3	76	7.6
3½	89	8.9
4	102	10.2
4½	114	11.4
5	127	12.7
6	152	15.2
7	178	17.8
8	203	20.3

Inches	Cm
9	22.9
10	25.4
11	27.9
12	30.5
13	33.0
14	35.6
15	38.1
16	40.6
17	43.2
18	45.7
19	48.3

Inches	Cm
20	50.8
21	53.3
22	55.9
23	58.4
24	61.0
25	63.5
26	66.0
27	68.6
28	71.1
29	73.7
30	76.2

INDEX